And the Penny Dropped

by R.L. Parks

Copyright © 2022 by R.L. Parks

All rights reserved. The use of any part of this publication, reproduced, transmitted in any form or by any means electronic, mechanical, photocopying, recording or otherwise, or stored in a retrieval system without permission in writing from the publisher—or in the case of photocopying or other reprographic copying, license from the Canadian Copyright Licensing agency—is an infringement of copyright law. Reviewers may quote brief passages in a review.

ISBN 978-1-7782446-0-5

Bicycle image by macrovector on freepik.com. Sky background image on cover by VecMes on freepik.com.

Cover and interior design by Melany Hallam, maywooddesign.com

"When someone is seeking" said Siddhartha, "it happens quite easily that he only sees the thing that he is seeking; that he is unable to find anything, unable to absorb anything, because he is only thinking of the thing he is seeking, because he has a goal, because he is obsessed with his goal... You, O worthy one, are perhaps indeed a seeker, for in striving towards your goal, you do not see many things that are under your nose."

HERMANN HESSE IN "SIDDHARTA"

[1982]

July 18

LEANNE'S NEW BOYFRIEND BROUGHT some friends camping with us this weekend. We were mid-party when they arrived and welcomed them with raised bottles and cheers. Not long after they'd joined us at the fire, I heard a sound coming from behind our van. Always on the alert for uninvited guests (especially the furry kind that like to sneak into warm sleeping bags), I asked what the tapping was. When I heard it was a woman named Jamie setting up her tent, I decided to offer her some help. It was so dark away from the fire that I couldn't see her face clearly but we chatted and worked together until it was done. Back in the light, I was surprised to see that she has a black patch over one eye.

We had a great time around the campfire - telling jokes and sharing funny stories. At one point, Jamie pulled out her guitar and sang a few songs. I was absolutely charmed. She's a tall woman with a strong, boyish body. She carries herself with unnerving confidence and speaks with the deep raspy voice of a man. She had the attention of every guy there, whether single, married, or long-time friend. She stood center stage and boy, did she have it down! We clicked in the humour department - howling about all our favourites from Bloom County and Saturday Night Live (What the hell is that?) I laughed so hard - beer came out of my nose.

July 19

This morning I crawled out of bed feeling a little less sure of myself than I did last night. Ouch! I made my way to the public washroom hoping I wouldn't bump into anyone before I had a chance to check myself in the mirror for the possibility of hair aerobics, mustard moustache (cold hot-dogs - ew), runaway nose hairs, or other facial embarrassments.

I was met by a line-up of other campers who unfortunately didn't have that after-the-party look. A memory of people angrily complaining about our noise flashed in my mind. As I stood there reeking of stale alcohol, cigarette smoke, and other enjoyable substances, I wished I could forget. Who needs guilt when you feel like somebody did the inside of your mouth in wall-to-wall shag? While fighting the urge to bulldoze everyone between me and the sink, I realized that I couldn't remember what Jamie looked like. I thought I could recognize her voice and tuned my ears to the annoying hum around me. Damn that was painful; had to tune out again. Shut up, will ya?

When I got back to the campsite, Tim was awake and steaming mad. He said I'd treated him like a pervert. He woke me up for sex two hours after I'd gone to bed wasted with the spins. I hadn't said a word, hadn't gotten angry - just pushed him off me, rolled over and went back to sleep. I asked him how that was treating him like a pervert. He wanted to know why I'd taken off before he woke up. I had to pee. I needed water. I needed a toothbrush. I thought I was being considerate by being careful not to wake him up. Did I leave to avoid sex? No. Did I want sex? No. It seems I have a growing list of times I don't want sex: when I'm feeling crappy in the middle of the night, first thing in the morning when my head is pounding with a hangover, and when my supposed boyfriend doesn't give two hoots whether I'm in the mood or not. I couldn't believe he was so hurt and angry because I wouldn't have sex when I felt like crap. It made me mad and I thought about all the times I'd had sex with him when I wasn't in the mood and he hadn't even noticed. And that made me feel madder but also kind of sad. It was too much to think about - and there was no way I was going to drive all the way home with him shouting at me - so I caught a ride with Jamie and the guys. I couldn't help feeling sorry for Tim - and the cheerful chatter and singing were a little hard to take at first - but I eventually relaxed and enjoyed the ride. I know Tim and I are done, but I have a strong feeling that things are moving in the right direction.

August 16

I moved into Jamie's place three weeks ago. Her folks are away until the end of September. It's so much fun and her friends are great! We party at night and hang out in the sun during the day. Yesterday afternoon, Jamie decided she was going to give us all a good soaking. As she bent over the garden to turn on the hose, Kirsten snuck up and held the nozzle under Jamie's butt. Was she surprised!! It was war after that…

Jamie is hilarious. She walks around her backyard and picks up the dead mice that her cats have abandoned, swings them around by the tail, and tosses them over the hedge into the neighbours yard! I keep expecting to hear a shriek one day when an unsuspecting gardener gets a mouse in the side of the head. But it hasn't happened yet and it probably never will. Jamie gets away with so many things like that. If I did it once, I'd probably get caught and run out of town.

I love sitting on Jamie's back porch listening to her play guitar and sing tunes like Neil Young's "Old Man". She's the first musician I've ever met and my admiration goes beyond the fact that I'm tone deaf. She moves me, in a way that few people have. Ya ya, everything moves me, I cry at commercials, but this is different. She's different; she makes me feel free.

The other night we were sitting around playing a drinking game with Kim, Jenn & Trish. I've known Jamie for less than a month, and she's known the others for less than that. Out of the blue, she says, "Do you guys masturbate?" I nearly spewed my drink across the room. I'd never heard that word spoken aloud when it wasn't part of a joke or teasing. Of course everyone was surprised and either squeaked out a defensive "no" or sat with their mouths gaping. Jamie didn't believe anyone and let us know it. She's a no BS girl, and clearly thinks it's stupid to be afraid to talk about such things. I've also realized that she enjoys shocking people…

It's great to finally have someone to really talk to. We talk about books and movies, and experiences with other people. She told me she got caught reading "The Happy Hooker" when she was 11. She covers details that blow my mind. She answers all the questions I've been too embarrassed to ask. She makes sex seem natural and not dirty like I obviously thought it was. Sometimes I feel embarrassed at how interested I am in talking about it. Even that makes me feel weird, but not for long. Jamie likes talking about sex and never lets on if she notices my awkwardness. I think she likes feeling like my big sister, though she's two years younger. Jamie's whole family is pretty relaxed. I was surprised to see pictures of them naked by a lake when they were young. At my house, you don't leave your room without a housecoat on (and I'm okay with that).

We party a lot. Jamie always knows how to have fun. During our house parties, we attack each other when least expected - like Cato and Inspector Clouseau. I'll be walking down the hall and suddenly Jamie will pounce out of nowhere and we'll be rolling on the ground wrestling and laughing our heads off. We sit on each other's laps, sharing drinks and cigarettes, and jokes that no one else can understand. We join everyone in drinking games and go from playing caps in the kitchen, to Salute in the living room. Salute is such a funny game. Jamie always comes up with the best actions and the toughest rules. When you have to remember all 14 actions on top of not being able to point, say someone's name, or swear, you're bound to get drunk - and, of course, that's her not-so-secret plan.

One night, Jamie, her cousin (wee Jamie), and I played a drinking game with a pack of Chippendale cards and a big bottle of Champagne. That was the first time we had a group bubble bath - and it was the first time I'd met wee Jamie! So much for formalities... Before long, we were assigning titles for our newly created "Norby Nipple Club" (norby is a Jamie word for huge). I believe someone said that mine looked like a mistake: "Oops, wrong size… oh well." Someone else said that it looked as though my breasts had just never caught up. I wasn't offended by these fairly accurate remarks. In fact, it's Jamie who is president, not I. Now Jamie initiates bubble bath parties amongst our girlfriends. Jamie's friends are all like her; they aren't shy about their bodies at all. So there we are, 3 or 4 girls at a time, sitting in a big old claw foot tub, legs hanging over the side, bubbles everywhere, beers and wine glasses, cigarettes and doobies, a ghetto-blaster on the floor playing our favourite tunes... And I always feel the same way - like I've died and gone to a really good party!

There's nothing sexual about these parties, although the men we hang out with want to think so. One guy in particular has a hard time with it. He's sure that Jamie and I are gay. He thinks the way we act at parties and how affectionate we are means that we're lovers. He's wrong. It bothers me that he feels like that. He's mean sometimes and makes cracks in front of other people. Jamie doesn't give a damn. She rarely cares what people think. But I don't want people to think that about us. I'm crazy about Jamie, but Rick's suggestions that we're sleeping together make me feel weird. I hate him being around. I like things the way they are, and I don't want him messing with that. I want it to go on forever.

November 7

I had to tell Jamie about my affair with Hailey. Why? Because before I met her, I got drunk and confessed to the wrong person. I didn't have a god to punish me so I told the biggest blabbermouth I knew, who claimed to be my best friend BUT once the cat was out of the bag, "Well Riley, if you turn out to be gay, I don't think we can be friends because we'll have nothing in common." Ouch! But hey, not such a big deal because if I know one thing, I know that I'm not gay. It was a phase, a drunken error in judgement - and hey, she jumped me! It was... never mind. I lost 15 pounds in two weeks (from "freaking"), and got beat up by Jason (the jealous boyfriend). He didn't even know we'd been together; he just turned on me when I tried to stop him from planting her skull in the pavement outside a bar.

And that brings us to the SHOCKING news that made headlines this week in the world of prefersnottobenoticedforprettymuch anything Riley (yes as much as I wish it weren't, that's me): My big-mouthed PAL informed ALL of my other friends that I prefer women to men – HEY I NEVER SAID THAT – AND I WAS DRUNK EVERY TIME!! Too late, I'm a rumour. I guess I don't handle being a rumour very well. A few nights ago, while Jamie was out on a doobie run and I was wasted, I went into her backyard with a steak knife and started sawing at my wrist. It was dark in the yard and silent. I cried into the shadows and kept looking at the house. The lights were on inside. I thought of home. I thought of Mom, Dad, and the boys. I realized I couldn't do it – again. I cried in Jamie's arms for a long, long time that night. I felt foolish the next day and extremely tired and weak. Jamie comforted and encouraged me. She told me she'd had a crush on her best friend when she was 11 and had kissed her. I admitted that I'd kissed my best friend in grade 7. "Lots of people have those experiences," she assured me. "And you know what?" she added, "Being gay is okay too. Screw anybody who has a problem with it." "But I'm not gay," I said. "Okay," she smiled, and hugged me again. I feel like she's the only one on my side and I love her more. She told me not to worry about what other people think and reminded me that when the smoke clears, I'll know who my real friends are. When the rumours continued to fly about the two of us, she egged everyone on by being even more affectionate and attentive with me.

 Yesterday, I found myself out shopping for a mini-skirt with her. Yes – me in a skirt! We got all dolled up and went downtown with Jamie's sister who's visiting from up north and was in serious need of some dancing.

 Before we went over the bridge into town, we stopped to pick up some pot and smoked a joint for the road. So there we were, three women in a two-seated van, stereo cranked, swilling beer and enjoying our buzz, laughing and chatting up a storm. We came flying around the bend at the entrance to the bridge…and damn – a roadblock… "Put down the beers"! But it was too late; they were looking right at us. Reeking of pot and beer, no seat belts, open liquor in the car, and oops – at least a half dozen empties hit the road when they slid open the side door. "Those are from our camping trip last weekend, really!" And then I splashed the officer's boots when he told me to pour out the rest of the beer... Jamie said she didn't know whether to thank God or the mini-skirts but we walked away with a warning and a "Have a good evening girls." Phew! So we danced on the tables and had a hell of a good time.

This morning, I was awoken by Jamie's sister standing over our sleeping bags in the basement. I was all tangled up in the shredded t-shirt Jamie lent me. I asked her for a whole t-shirt, but she said she'd cut 'em all up after she saw Flashdance. So there I was, tied up in knots, my head threatening to explode all over the room (Whose coke was that anyway?) and Jamie's sister was trying to talk Jamie into having a shower with her. What? It almost woke me up completely. When I asked her about it later, she said her family took showers together sometimes, ever since her Dad built the shower in the basement and they'd all had a shower together to christen it. I started to wonder whose family was unusual - hers or mine?

[1987]

August 9

IT'S BEEN A LONG time since I picked this up but I'm so glad I did. Reading about that summer with Jamie, I can't help smiling. We were bad back then, but it was so much fun. Things changed when Jamie got a boyfriend and I got busy with school, but a bond had formed between us that'll never be broken. Jamie held a mirror up for me that gave me a glimpse of who I might be beyond rules, imagined expectations, and fear of judgement. Through her example, I realized that it's not all black and white – that there are a lot of different ways of being and it is for me to decide what suits me. She also showed me wonderful things about myself that made me want to be stronger and know who I really am. Realizing that I might not be weird after all, a door opened. She made me crave the freedom of not caring what people think of me. I might dance and sing – and strut naked and unashamed... Someday I will. Jamie made it seem possible. She'll be forever in my ear, coaching me, daring me...

September 12

Ever since Elizabeth died, I can't stop thinking about what happened. I feel so different, like I have a new goal but I don't know exactly what it is yet. More than anything, I hope I can hold on to the sense of peace it gave me (weird as that sounds). I know I really don't have the words but I'm going to try to write it down.

Mom called me at Jamie's to tell me about Elizabeth. I shouldn't have driven because I cried the whole way and my vision was blurry – but I just wanted to be home. Mom and dad were sitting in the back yard. It was sunny and warm. Mom spoke softly when she explained about the clot. They wanted me to sit with them, but I couldn't. I went to my room and crawled under the covers. I couldn't remember feeling so ripped open before, so raw. I had never cried so hard. I kept thinking of her – singing her good morning song to wake me up, sitting with me while I ate the breakfast she'd made for me, telling me stories of her childhood on the prairies, driving me to work... Every Saturday morning for more than two years, while Donna slept and my mom was miles away, Elizabeth treated me like one of her own. And I loved her for it.

I kept thinking of Donna and Megan without their mom, Harold without his wife – and I cried so hard my insides hurt. I'd been swallowed up in a dark and painful place from which I'd never escape. Nothing would ever be the same. The pain would never end. I cried myself to sleep.

I woke up hours later and rolled onto my back. My room was full of light, though the blind was open and it was dark outside. I felt the most incredible sense of peace, a lightness I could never describe, warmth, love. I turned over and fell instantly back to sleep.

In the morning, I still felt filled with the most calming light and kind of happy to be honest. Mom and Dad didn't say anything but I know they were worried about me and probably thought I'd gone into shock or something. When I thought of Elizabeth, I still felt sad, but it wasn't devastating and it didn't have the crushing weight that it had the night before. I didn't cry again until the funeral. I wasn't shut off – I just knew that she was okay and that we'd all be okay too. I decided not to tell Donna about it but I thought Elizabeth must have visited me – to let me know that she was okay. Whatever happened, a door has been opened and I feel curious and ready to walk through it.

[1988]

December 29

I WANT TO WRITE about what happened this year so that I never forget it. The course was mind-blowing. So many bizarre experiences, insights, and shifts in perspective ... Sometimes I'm surprised I still recognize myself. I guess I just know myself better. But not completely and that's another reason I want to write this down. Maybe it'll help me figure out what I've been avoiding.

When Deb told me about the private Transformational Therapy program that she was taking, I could hardly wait until the next session began. Deb and I have always been on the same page when it comes to pondering the meaning of life. We're both hungry for answers and excited by the mysteries in the world that might hold them. Throughout high school, we spent many nights talking into the wee hours and pouring over books on archaeology, philosophy, and spirituality. While being with Jamie makes me feel normal and free, talking with Deb makes me feel sane. We spent less time together as I looked for self esteem in my new party crowd and she moved into the university scene.

Not long after Elizabeth died, I came across Shirley MacLaine's book, "Out on a Limb". I cried when I read it. My experience with Elizabeth awoke my curiosity about a realm I'd barely thought about before. Shirley MacLaine inspired me to consider possibilities and made me realize I was, in some way, on a spiritual journey of my own. I felt compelled to reconnect with Deb and discuss the book with her. We met for lunch and that's when Deb told me about the therapist program.

Three times a year, the instructor (Nadja) took on a small group of students. My 8-month intensive program began in May when Deb was half way through hers. The approach we learned was based in Transpersonal Psychology. We studied the concepts of the persona (the part of yourself you present to others) and the shadow (the part of yourself you judge and hide, even from yourself) proposed by Carl Jung. We read "No Boundary" by Ken Wilber, "The Uses of Enchantment" by Bruno Bettelheim, and so on. We learned counselling techniques from various theoretical traditions including regression, visualization, meditation, and the interpretation of interpersonal dynamics, projection, and dreams. It was fascinating – and challenging.

Like most counsellors in training, we were required to experience the techniques and examine our own issues and relationship dynamics. I think the greatest benefit was taking on a perspective that fostered compassion for myself and others. I began to see the unconscious pain, fears, and misconceptions that sometimes influence behaviour, especially patterns that lead people into the same situations again and again.

A few weeks into the training, Nadja turned our attention toward our body chemistry, asking us to notice familiar sensations in our bodies that arose with particular emotions and thoughts. It was interesting. She also taught us (through experience) how to guide clients through a regression (following the sensations to a source in the past). The process usually resulted in some pretty amazing insights (and healing) regarding pain and struggles in the present. Sometimes, the regressions led to such painful memories that the process came to an abrupt halt. In those cases, the person was encouraged to try again when they felt ready. Nadja believes that pain is energy that is trapped in the body and that we suffer it again and again in different versions of the same story until we heal (e.g. a battered child who grows up to become a battered wife). If we don't heal, the pain energy may become toxic and cause illness or disease.

One weekend during the program, I went to a party. At some point during the evening, a horrible (and very familiar) sensation arose. It was still lingering when I arrived in class on the Monday, so I decided to look at it. I call it "the mire" – because it feels like a dark, sickening ooze that creeps through my body, making me want to crawl out of my own skin. It sometimes moves into my mind, bringing dark, suicidal thoughts that have to be wrestled and pushed away. It used to leave bruises sometimes, but I've gotten better at resisting that. Too many questions and too many lies. Drinking less and cutting out the hard drugs has helped.

In an attempt to help me understand the mire, Nadja asked me to find the feeling in my body and make it bigger. Then she asked questions designed to draw out unconscious connections, memories, knowledge, etc. Through this process, I came to recognize the mire as a feeling of shame and self-disgust. A few memories of self-injury surfaced, including the night I cut my wrist in Jamie's backyard, but that was as far as I got. Nadja was soon guiding me outside – literally – because I couldn't breathe. My chest was so constricted that I was gasping for air. I felt like I was going to suffocate.

I didn't want to try again after that. My body told me I wasn't ready – and I believed it. Besides, I was managing. Ever since I stopped myself that night at Jamie's and then even more so since my experience when Elizabeth died, the battle has been much easier. I haven't been able to stop the mire from arising completely, but it comes less often and it's weaker. I don't feed the dark thoughts with possibility. I keep choosing life and positive thoughts about myself. Nadja helped me with that too. She introduced me to my higher (spirit) self, the wise part of myself, to which I can turn for guidance and strength at any time.

I learned a lot about myself during the course. Some of it was liberating, and some of it was really hard to face. I came to see that I was still terrified of judgement and frequently betrayed myself in pursuit of acceptance and validation. I was afraid that if people knew who I really was, they would reject me. The paradox was that even I didn't know who I really was...

Toward the end of the program, I had a dream that my hands and feet were on fire. I woke myself up trying to shake off the flames. I walked into class the next day, still carrying the horrible feeling of the dream in my body. When I said I didn't really have anything to share in the opening circle, everyone laughed. Denial and attempts at avoidance never worked in that class. In fact, they pretty much guaranteed you were going to be the focus for the session. Nadja guided me through an exploration of the images and feelings of the dream. She asked me to close my eyes and pay attention to where the disturbing feeling was in my body. She said to focus on it and allow it to grow. I remember it as a sickening mixture of fear, pain, and anger. Nadja gently guided me through the process of expanding the emotions, and then she asked, "If you knew when you first experienced these feelings, when would it have been?"

And then I was suddenly somewhere else, hands and feet bound, something rigid behind my back. Smoke and heat and pain. Eyes burning, lungs burning, skin burning, tears burning, rage burning. I came back to the room almost instantly – shocked by the experience. "Joan of Arc," Nadja whispered and I nodded, as if possessed by someone who knew what was happening, while I hid in a corner of myself, totally confused and overwhelmed.

"You were enraged," Nadja commented.

"Yes," I said.

"Who were you so angry with?" Nadja asked.

"A man – I don't know who he was, but I hate him," I replied. "WHO DO YOU THINK YOU ARE?" I heard myself roar inside my head, "WHO ARE YOU TO JUDGE ME?"

"You also seemed very sad," Nadja said.

"Yes," responded the informed part of myself, "Because he wasn't there."

"Who wasn't there?" Nadja prodded.

"God," said the part of me that didn't seem to know I didn't believe in a god, "He said he would be there and he wasn't." Tears came then and I cried myself into exhaustion. No more images, no more thoughts, and the anger gave way to a great heavy sadness.

I was pretty freaked out by the time I got home that evening, wondering if I'd really been Joan of Arc in a past life. I tossed and turned all night, my mind whirling. But I had an insight while I was out walking the next morning. It came to me that it wasn't important whether I actually had been Joan of Arc or not. I suddenly felt as though I "knew" that the energy of her life was in a kind of pool that any of us can draw from to learn about ourselves. When people die, the energy of their lives, and the lessons in them, become resources for us all. When we can't see where we are, they can provide us with insights. It's like identifying with a character in a book and understanding something about your own situation. Any number of people might identify with Joan of Arc and learn something about themselves by standing in her shoes for a moment. This calmed me and enabled me to focus on what was important.

I went to a library and read about Joan of Arc's life and death, looking for the gift of the regression. Though less intense, the anger from the regression surfaced when I read about the church sentencing the 19-year-old heroine to death. I also found myself wondering how she felt in the end. She believed that God led her into battle, that she was his servant. Then, she was burned at the stake for claiming that God spoke to her (through St. Michael, St. Catherine, and St. Margaret). "She must have felt betrayed by her country, the church, and perhaps even God," I decided. "And she must have been really pissed off," I thought, remembering the roar inside my head.

That week, Jamie did my Tarot. The centre card, which is the "heart of the matter" position (what you're dealing with), was the eight of swords (a woman blindfolded and bound). Though I wasn't familiar with Tarot at the time, I cried when I saw it. Jamie didn't have to tell me that it represented powerlessness – feeling victimized, persecuted. I was surprised when she read from her book that it also could mean 'being blind to freedom".

I discussed my feelings and insights with Nadja in a private session, but was unable to go any farther than acknowledging that the sadness and anger had something to do with me. Though I knew the anger was about judgement, I hit a brick wall when I tried to explore the connection to my own life. It felt like a tidal wave behind a door – and I didn't want to open it.

[1989]

February 4

I'M HOUSE-SITTING FOR NADJA, just up the street from Jamie. It's nice to be able to hang out with her more often again. We've grown up a bit and she's in a long-term relationship, but we still like to party and we can still make each other laugh. Last weekend, she introduced me to Kevin, a sexy mountain-man from New Zealand, who spends three quarters of the year in the bush with a geologist's crew. Jamie was the camp cook for his crew last summer. The night we met, Kevin didn't say much, but I liked his calm energy when we danced to a slow song. We went for a walk yesterday and I was surprised to see how much more outgoing he is away from the group. Though obviously a quiet man, he talks easily and has a good sense of humour. He stopped along our walk at one point and grabbed a handful of pine, rubbed it vigorously in his huge hands, and then held it up to his nose and took a deep breath. He seems kind and down-to-earth and healthy. Jamie thinks he's perfect. I think she's a bit jealous that he's interested in me.

April 15

It's only been 3 months and Kevin just asked me to move to New Zealand with him. I've been sitting here thinking about my feelings. Some part of me wants to be the person who moves off to New Zealand with the good-looking outdoorsman and lives happily ever after. But that's exactly the problem. Some part of me wants to be someone I'm not.

I like Kevin but I'm not in love with him. The more I get to know him, the more I think he wants a doting wife who has no life of her own. He gets upset when I want to spend time with friends – though I've hardly seen anyone since we met. I had to drag him to Gary's birthday party last night – and then on the way home he complained that I'd paid more attention to everyone else. I couldn't believe my ears! I'd spent the night feeling embarrassed because I wasn't paying attention to anyone but him. I was so worried about him feeling left out or upset that I'd let him keep me in his arms most of the night – standing on his feet! And that wasn't enough!

I am just not that girl. In fact, the more I think about it – it's like I've been impersonating someone else since I met him. Like I've been playing a role instead of being myself.

The truth is that there's no chemistry between us either. I felt it die when we slept together the first time. It feels like he's damaging my internal organs. So last week when I saw Dr. Bremer, I asked him if a man's size can be dangerous. He said that emotions trigger different kinds of hormones and that sex can be painful because I'm not relaxed. Who can relax when you're worried about your kidneys being relocated??

So that's that then. I'll talk to him tomorrow and then I'm taking a vow of celibacy. I've never been in love, never really enjoyed sex (even when organ relocation wasn't a concern), and I suck at relationships. If Kevin hadn't turned up the pressure, I probably would have gone on like this with him for a lot longer even though it obviously hasn't felt right. I did the same thing with Mark, Tim, and Jared. I'm not doing it anymore. Not a single date until I feel certain I'm attracted for the right reasons (to the person and not some picture) – and definitely no sex until I feel real desire. No more going along with it because that's what couples do. How stupid is that?

April 18

Jamie blew an absolute gasket when she heard I broke up with Kevin. She's decided that I'm gay and that's the reason that I dumped "the most perfect man on earth" – that she happens to have the hots for but never got into bed because I came along and screwed it all up! Well you can't sleep with everyone can you? And you have a boyfriend anyway so what else is new – thinking about cheating again – and I'M NOT GAY. And you used to be nicer. Now, you miss out on cheating with the mountain man and I'm a gay asshole. Thanks buddy...

I've never seen Jamie so angry (I now understand the expression "spitting mad") – and all because she thinks I'm "not admitting the truth to myself"? Even if that were true – and it's NOT – why would she be so mad? Screaming at me because she thinks I'm in denial? Really? Is it just because she has the hots for Kevin? Or is she in love with him? Either way, you think she'd be glad we broke up. His visa doesn't expire until January so now she has a chance if she wants it. That doesn't make any sense. What's it got to do with her? Does she feel bad because she introduced us? That doesn't really seem like her. Whatever it is she should figure out what this has to do with her and leave me alone. Maybe SHE'S gay! I'm not. I like men! I just haven't met the right one.

June 11

I'm going to Europe next spring! I've been thinking about this for a while and thought I'd go by myself, but I saw Jo last night and we decided to go together!

A little about Jo (Joanne): although she is someone I really like, we've only seen each other once a year since high school, usually at a reunion we organize after our Christmas card updates. She is one of the funniest people I know. She was the cooking class clown – eggs in your pockets, things in your soup... She was in the school annual at least twice every year – under her own name and an assumed name. How she came up with "Helga Zortenhoof" I'll never know. She can really make me laugh, so when she told me last night that she was also planning to go to Europe next year, I jumped at the chance to team up with her.

June 25

Jamie and I talked about Europe for years but I eventually came to believe that it wouldn't happen and had started making plans to go without her even before I saw Jo. Jamie has a boyfriend and money is tight as usual. But, when she heard that Jo and I had started planning our trip, she jumped on the bandwagon. She really wants to go and has talked us into making it a cycling trip. The fact that she is a bike courier, whereas I don't even own a bike didn't stop me from joining in the excitement of such an adventure. It hit me the other night when I was drinking with Donna and Gary. They nearly split themselves laughing when I told them I was going to cycle around Europe and I couldn't help but join in, laughing until I had tears in my eyes. What the hell have I signed up for?

July 15

I bought my mountain bike today! The guy talked me into an original, built by an Olympic cyclist friend of his. He assured me that it has the best of everything, at a much better price than if I went with a big name. I wasn't hard to convince. I don't know a thing about bikes. We have nine months to prepare, so I figure I can be ready. It is so exciting to have a new bike – I'm going to ride it as much as I can. Unfortunately, I won't be able to do any touring, but I can ride to work and do some off-road trail hopping. Hopefully that will get me in shape!

September 3

Jo, Jamie, and I had a great summer. We've planned our route, devoured travel books, learned how to change bike tires, and gone over our lists a zillion times. They even joined my baseball team and Jo came up with a name that I have a feeling will haunt us forever – Larry Loser. She was determined to make it our team name when we clearly deserved it, but the other players held onto their dignity. Did it stop there? Nope. From that point on the three of us were all Larry Losers and it grew to a no-turning-back-point one drunken night that I'm not allowed to talk about. It was engraved in stone after that ridiculous caper. We were officially: "Larry #1 – The Prez" (Jo), "Larry #2 – Vice President" (me), and "Larry #3 – Planner and Props Consultant" (Jamie). Last weekend, we went out and bought Bill the Cat t-shirts (in his oop-ack pose) and some t-shirt paint. Included in our elegant design is "LARRY" printed in huge letters on our backs, and of course our respective titles on the front. I'm so excited!!!!!!

[1990]

March 23

WE LEAVE FOR EUROPE one month from today. We're all out of shape from a lazy winter and a whole lot of partying. I can't believe that we're about to cycle our way across entire countries. It's surreal. Though definitely excited, I'm more than a little nervous and keep thinking, "What are we, nuts?" I smoke a pack of cigarettes a day, and I haven't had an hour of exercise in over 4 months...

Three things can not be long hidden: the sun, the moon, and the truth

BUDDHA

April 23

WE LANDED AT HEATHROW Airport just before noon, hangovers setting in with a vengeance and breath that arrived a little before we did. Jamie had spent the flight stealing mini bottles of wine from somewhere. Like they didn't notice we were wasted. If they'd missed Jo's "tour de plane", introducing herself to anyone who made the mistake of looking in her direction (she only spits a little when she slurs at ya), or the sound of her talking to the big white phone (oh excuse me I mean sink - she told us she had to scoop it into the toilet with paper towels because it wouldn't go down…thanks for that delightful anecdote Jo!), then they surely couldn't have missed it when she woke up the family sitting in front of us by pouring an entire drink down the man's back. I've never seen anyone jump like that. We voted that the most memorable moment thus far.

We all wore our Larry Loser t-shirts for the flight and had lots of comments from passengers and staff: "Who's Larry?" "Hey Larry". An English fellow at Heathrow asked Jamie if she was in a band. Probably that new perm…

The customs dude made the mistake of giving me a bad time - questioning my intentions in England, demanding my money so he could count it. Didn't he realize I hadn't had any sleep? Couldn't he smell me? Didn't he sense danger in the redness of my eyes and the chaos of my hair? Lucky for him, Jo saw the storm brewing and intervened. We managed to get out of there without any casualties.

Jamie's dad's cousin, John, picked us up at the airport in a van. We threw the bikes and gear in the back, and Jo and I gratefully passed out on the floor. About half an hour later we woke up to John cursing the absence of a turnaround in the highway. Why do we need to turn around?? Well, turns out Larry #3 forgot her bag in the parking lot. No big deal, it just had her passport, all her ID, and all her money... Fortunately, the day was saved by an honest person and she was able to retrieve it at the lost and found. Phew!!

So here we are in London, all snuggled up in bed, writing in our journals. We did it!! We finally made it!!! Jamie's relatives seem really nice. I might even forgive them for serving me scrambled eggs – yuck! Time to sleep now. It may be the first day of my dream come true, but it's been awfully long.

April 24

We all woke up early to the rustle of sleeping bags...rustle, rustle...rustle. "Hey! Keep it down willya Larry, I'm tryin' to sleep." A pillow to the head and a "Yo Russell" started the day with a laugh and we jumped into gear. Lookout London, the Larry Losers are in town! John asked us what the Larry Loser club was, but it was hard to explain how we all became Larry and how we're proud to be Larry Losers. It's a weird humour thing that the three of us have in common. Larry's kind of like a Ziggy – everything happens to Larry and Larry happens to everyone. Larry's doing Europe, that's the scoop. Oh well, so it's a little weird. It's Jo's influence. She's the Prez after all.

Downtown London is wild. Busy, crowded, and insane drivers. Yikes! I was just saying to Jamie that we'd better watch out for the traffic when I was nearly honked out of my shoes by a cab that only missed me because I made a dive for the sidewalk. Some construction workers asked me if I was o.k. I was awake that's for sure!!

It was a great day. We tripped around town (sometimes literally – "Piss off Jamie"), and did the sightseeing thing: wore some pigeons at Trafalgar Square, gawked at the guards at Buckingham Palace, did some bus surfing on the upper level of a double-decker (people smoke on the bus here!), and left our John Henry's (Larry Loser's actually) in the guest register at the Canadian Embassy. Jo

& Jamie nearly wrecked the place on the way in. I don't know what they were doing to the door, but the security guard almost had a seizure. Jamie politely suggested that he "Take a pill". I pretended not to know them...

Tonight, John took us to visit Jamie's aunt that she hadn't seen since she was five. John wanted it to be a surprise, so he pushed Jamie up front when her aunt opened the door. She was really nervous and John, Jo, and I nearly peed ourselves laughing when she said, "Hi, I'm your nephew Jamie." Other quotes of the day include: Jo to me - "It's neat how they say "bloats", I'll have to write that in my postcard." Me - "What's a bloat?" Jo - "You know, a chap." Me - "That's a bloke you loser." And later, Jo on the subway - "That station was called Way out" ("Way out" means "exit"). What a Larry!

London is cool, but it's really polluted. My face was filthy after an hour in town and when we got back - I blew black stuff out of my nose! I even saw some bike couriers wearing gas masks!! I'd never ride my bike in London - it's scary enough walking... Well, time to write a few postcards and then try to sleep through the rustling of losers.

April 25th

We must have slept like logs last night because the first thing I heard was John bringing in a tray of tea at 9 am (what a sweetie). So up for tea, a bath, and downstairs for a breakfast of toast, sausage, & tomatoes. Then, into London with a picnic lunch.

We went to St. Paul's Cathedral first. It's really something! The original cathedral was built on the same spot in 604 AD, but it was destroyed. The current cathedral is almost 300 years old. The paintings, sculptures, and stained glass would take hours to truly appreciate the detail. The tombs were also magnificent. I found myself really taken with a display portraying the place where Christ moved the rock and left his burial place. It made me feel strange - kind of relieved. I don't know why. I guess the idea of rebirth is appealing (in the butterfly rather than angel sense that is). I feel like I need to change or evolve in a significant way. And this trip feels like a new beginning, a chance to break free... Of what, I haven't a clue.

Jo paid to climb the 627 steps to the upper level but Jamie and I decided to ranch on the lawn and people-watch for a while. I eavesdropped, loving the English accents. I wonder what a Canadian sounds like to them? Can't possibly be as cool.

We took the bus to the Tower of London next. It's a castle (made up of several towers) that was built for William the Conqueror almost 1000 years ago. It houses museums, the crown jewels, and the old and new armouries. My first feeling at the sight of the castle was awe – at the architecture and the centuries of time the Tower had witnessed. Second, was an eerie feeling because of the violence that took place there. Noticing the slits in the exterior walls for firing arrows, the cannons, drawbridge, guard towers, and huge spiked gates before we went inside, I started to imagine the time and it gave me the shivers. Once inside, the feeling magnified with the stories of Henry the VIII. During his reign, the Tower of London was used as a prison and place of execution for several people out of Henry's favour, including Sir Thomas More and Anne Boleyn, Henry's second wife. Supposedly because she wasn't producing a son, Anne Boleyn was set up and wrongly convicted of adultery, incest, and plotting to kill the king. That in mind, I was surprised to learn that she made a speech at her execution, announcing that her punishment was just and asking for God's blessing on King Henry. Perhaps she considered her crime marrying Henry in the first place...

While we stood next to the Tower Green, where the chopping block had been, a tour guide pointed out The Bloody Tower where two young princes had been murdered because they were heirs to the throne after their father, Edward IV, died. It was never proven, but their uncle and protector, Richard III, was suspect because he pronounced himself king a month later. Before those cheerful images had passed, the guide turned to point out the Queen's House, where the ghost of Arbella Stuart supposedly walks the halls.

Before I had a chance to ask who Arbella Stuart was (and whether she was a friendly sort of ghost), Jamie dragged us off to the display of torture and execution instruments. From there, I was dragged by two excited (and twisted if you ask me) Larrys to the White Tower. They had decided to look for a dungeon... We crept around inside the White Tower looking for a door that would lead us down into a dungeon. Seems creeping is not a Larry's best thing (slightly obvious)... But they finally picked a door. "That's got to be it," Jo assured us. We waited until the coast was clear and then just as we were about to go for it, a guard came through the door. We gave up after that. "Good one Jo, it probably leads to the staff room..."

A bit later, Jo and I hid around a corner from where Jamie was picking at the stone wall, trying to get a souvenir. We pulled our t-shirts up over our heads so we'd look beheaded. We were giggling because we couldn't see anything and we could hear people laughing as they passed by. What the hell was taking her so long? I looked around the corner four times thinking she was coming. If I didn't know better, I'd have thought it was a plot to "add humour" to my hair as I pulled my t-shirt up and down a dozen times trying to see where she was. Needless to say, Jo and I were rather disappointed when Jamie finally came around the corner and said, "Oh look, a couple of ghosts" as she walked right by. How do I let Jo talk me into these ridiculous things?

Somehow Jamie and I lost Jo on the way back to John and Claire's. We made our way onto a crowded subway and did our sardine impersonations while I fought waves of claustrophobia. I wonder how many Canadians don't even realize they're claustrophobic? The London Underground at rush hour is a sure fire way to find out. Believe me! If you're still not sure then wait until the train stops for a while - in a dark tunnel - under the city... And then, just when you think you've got yourself under control - the lights go out... Great, just great! I had to ask Jamie to talk to me to get my mind off it. How could she be so cool? I felt like punching her.

Well, we survived and made it home to tell the tale. John and Claire are such great people. They're always anxious to hear about our adventures and we have a lot of laughs together. Tonight we went out to the neighbourhood pub with them. It was packed and most people seemed to know each other. I was surprised to see a few kids in there - not drinking of course. We had a good time, and laughed all the way home.

By the time we go to bed, I feel so wound up from laughing with everyone that I can't get to sleep, no matter how exhausted I am. Sleeping between cousin Rustle and cousin Snore doesn't help either. How the hell does Jamie fall asleep so fast and what does Jo do in that sleeping bag?? When I came out of the bathroom, on my way to bed, I heard Claire call John a "bloat" and they giggled together.

Quote of the day: The last Larry in the bathroom (not mentioning any names) calls out, "It smells like fish in here"... gales of laughter... and then with a tone of defensive embarrassment, slightly quieter than the first announcement, "Well it does." More laughter. Well it did.

April 26

Today we put our bikes together. Hauled the boxes out of the basement and went to work in the backyard. It's almost time to go, only a couple more days!! We had a bit of a rough start. I hope it's no indication of how our trip is going to go. We were all feeling pretty cocky, what with our fancy mountain bikes, tools and gear ... our big cycle Europe plan. I couldn't help feeling kinda cool, y'know? But cool went right out the window when I swung my leg over my bike for the first time and stuck my foot in a big empty diaper box, lost my balance, knocked a bunch of pails over, and almost fell into a big tub of green stuff. Oh thank god I didn't fall into that green stuff. Of course everyone saw the whole thing and howled with laughter. Even I couldn't control myself - what a goof. And I wasn't the only Larry on a bike today. We finally got started and not even a half a block from the house, I pulled over to do up my jacket and Jo, who didn't see me stop, rode right into me, caught her handlebar in my jacket and fell over her bike! God did we laugh about that... to tears.

Jamie's mom's brother and his wife came over to visit and we played the Pictionary game we bought John and Claire for a thank you gift. John warned us about Uncle Gordon's eyebrows but I still couldn't help jumping back a bit. Whoa, tame those things will ya? Aunt Doris brought out some pictures of their new grandson in the hospital. In one of the pics, the baby had socks on his hands and Jo whispered to me, "Poor little guy, looks like he had to do a puppet show." We got into a pretty serious goonie hour after that and spent the rest of the night wiping tears from our eyes. The night ended with Jamie letting a big ripper go on the porch and blaming me as the living room broke up in laughter. Thanks friend.

April 27

We headed out in a rush this morning to go to Stonehenge. We hopped off the bus when we saw a sign that said subway. Running like mad fools, we raced in one entrance and came out on the other side of the street. Huh? Back in again and out yet another side. Okay, you go that way, you go that way, and I'll go this way. Waving stupidly from opposite corners of the street, we realized a subway is a pedestrian underpass. So the race was on. We ran to the nearest station, stopping for directions once in a while, letting Jo (the non-smoker) ask while we tried not to cough up a lung. For all our efforts and sweat, we still missed the bus. Damn! I really wanted to go to Stonehenge and now we won't have time. Jamie said she didn't really care; she thinks it's BS that it's covered with plastic and roped off now. Could it be that too many people were taking chunks of it home for souvenirs Larry?

We ended up going to Covent Garden, though we never did find the garden... Well it's caaalled a garden, don't you think there'd beee a garden? Anyway it was fun. We watched a comedian in the square while we ate the lunch Claire packed for us, and then we went to a pub. A man in his seventies chatted us up, flirting, making jokes and asking us for our bear stories. Everybody wants to hear bear stories. Lucky for them Jamie knows a ton from her days as a bush cook. How in the world someone as bearanoid as her ended up as a bush cook, I'll never know. She's an awesome camper but in the bush she freaks at even the slightest sound. "It's a bear." "It's just the wind Jamie." "It's a bear." "It's just a bird Jamie." "It's a bear." "It's just me Jamie"…

    I told the story of our camping trip up in the Squamish Valley. Jamie took Andrea, Helene, and I to a great little spot they'd found on Ashlu creek. We pulled up in Jamie's little red car, singing Love Shack by the B52s, cold beers already cracked. We left the car doors open as we got out to find a good place for our tents. Jamie wandered into a grassy area away from the creek. I was looking at her, facing into the bush, when she jumped a foot and then started running in my direction. I can't remember if anyone said anything; I just remember running as fast as I could back to the car, knowing we were all running, and then there we were: sitting in the car, in our exact same seats no doubt, beers still in hand, huffing and puffing, and sweating to death because the windows had been quickly rolled up and now it was scorching inside. The sun was beating down on us. It must've been 200 degrees in there. We cracked up the second we relaxed – at the sight of us melting away in the car and the fact that we'd all managed to hold onto our beers. Jamie insisted that although she hadn't actually seen the bear, she'd definitely heard one growl at her from the bushes. Definitely. Hmmm.

    Later that same weekend, we hiked out to some sand dunes along the river. A totally cool spot where Ashlu creek meets the Squamish River. There was a big waterfall just across the river and the mountain views were beautiful. The dunes are so cool. Smooth white sand for running, diving, and sinking your feet into. We followed deer and cougar tracks, half naked and dancing with spears. We played badminton and Land, a game Jamie taught us. I wanted to stay there forever, our own private paradise. How great it feels to have the sun on your skin and the sand under your bare feet, while you listen to the river rush by. We tried swimming but it was quick - brrr… "C'mon ya wimps, it's not that cold," Jamie said. No? Instant high beams if you know what I mean.

Suddenly, huge dark clouds came over the mountain and we knew it was going to dump – and soon. We reluctantly headed back toward the campsite. It started pouring before we'd even gotten off the dunes so we made a run for the trees but got drenched anyway. We were making our way through some pretty dense brush when everyone stopped dead in their tracks. Andrea, who'd been leading the way, pointed at a tree jutting out of some brush just a few yards ahead. The tree was swaying violently back and forth. It was pouring rain but it wasn't windy. None of the other trees were moving at all. Just as my brain was processing the fact that it would take something pretty big to move that tree like that, Jamie blew her whistle in my ear – full bloody tilt! We all jumped a foot this time and I nearly had a heart attack. It scared the life right out of me. Really! Before I could recover, the others started moving again, making noise to let whatever was shaking that tree know we were moving away from it, and scrambling to get across the creek as quickly as possible. We lost our way in our hurry and couldn't find the fallen tree we'd used to cross the creek that stood between us and the main trail. We had to backtrack past the swaying tree again, but I was too worried about the ringing in my ear and wondering if I was deaf, to care about some stupid bear. "Jesus Jamie, you blew it right in my ear." I couldn't believe she'd done that. We finally got across and carried on, talking as loud as we could so the bears could hear us over the pounding rain.

 We startled a couple making out in their 4 x 4 when we fell out of the brush onto a dirt road. It must've been quite the sight: four soaking wet women sporting giant grins and badminton racquets, suddenly stumble out of the bush, laughing and tripping over one another, spot the observers, laugh harder, and then tip-toe into the bush on the other side of the road and disappear. Just when you thought you were alone…

April 28

Today was great! My best day yet. I headed into London by myself to join a march I saw advertised on the subway. It was a protest against vivisection. "World day for laboratory animals." I arrived at Battersea Park before the march started so I sat down on my sweater to watch the crowd and take a picture. While I was admiring all the people who came out with their dogs, I was approached by one of those tiny little things with long hair. I smiled at him and told him how cute he was, but he obviously wasn't impressed. He peed on my sweater! I couldn't believe it! What a brat! Jeez.

I joined the march when it started and it was wonderful. I just love marching with people. I was an ear-to-ear grin as we flowed through the streets of London. The strength of all these loving people was empowering. People of all walks of life, united together in a common cause. They chanted: "No more torture, no more lies, every 6 minutes an animal dies." "What do we want? Animal liberation! When do we want it? Now! Are we gonna fight for it? Yes. Are we gonna get it? Yes!" "Human freedom, animal rights, one battle, one fight!" The voices of the crowd belonged to adults and children of all ages. A boy of about 10 led the chants for my section of the walk with a megaphone. Looking at him and his belief that he could make a difference choked me up. It felt so good to be a part of it. At one point, we passed three elderly women standing outside their car, waving at the marchers. They had their hands over their hearts and tears in their eyes. I thought they were beautiful. And later, when it was over and I was walking to the station, I passed a man who was probably in his 70's, walking along smiling and singing, "No more torture, no more lies,..." Adorable!

It's weird how easy it is for us to live in denial about the grim realities we participate in: Animal lovers purchase products tested on animals; parents purchase products that are the result of child labour; everyone participates in the destruction of our one and only planet; and our governments feed the wealth (and therefore power) of corrupt and oppressive rulers. I have to admit that I'm guilty of the denial myself. If I think about the pollution caused by the transportation of my favourite imported foods... never mind the packaging production and disposal (years to breakdown if ever and then the earth has absorbed what??) or the fact that the people who work the hardest at the production end are probably barely able to feed their families.

This march was good for me. Aside from the wake-up call, it was good to go off on my own. It gave me confidence to go into London by myself and I had such a great day. I went home feeling happy, strong and excited about the rest of the trip.

We went to the pub tonight and it was weird. For the past week, I've been having a good time, but I'm always worried about what everyone thinks of me. I notice myself going to extremes to present and protect a certain picture of myself. I can't handle to think someone has the wrong idea about me. I did some positive affirmations and I feel a little better now. The hardest part seems to be not judging myself for judging myself - god!

Tomorrow is the BIG DAY! We're hitting the road!

April 29

Well we did it. We survived the first day - and rode about 40 miles! It was hell. We started out in weird moods that sucked up our energy. Jamie and I had had bad dreams. I dreamt a friend died and she dreamt she had cancer and couldn't go on the trip. Just fear I guess. The teary good-bye to John and Claire didn't help and the weather was grey and dismal (the outside looks like the inside I thought). Once we started moving, some of the excitement of the adventure kicked in and I felt my energy level rise. All decked out in our riding duds, gear strapped to the back of our bikes... we headed through London into the unknown. A real adventure! Yeah that's right - through London. But it wasn't that bad actually, being a Sunday and early (8:30 am) - it was dead. We pretty much had the streets to ourselves.

John and Claire escorted us out to our starting point and then we had the map that they'd helped us trace our first day on. We were headed toward Oxford and from the point they left us at it should've been clear sailing. "Should've been" but "wasn't." We were supposed to be headed west from the south end of our map. After a good hour of riding and still not finding the highway, we stopped someone on the street for directions. I asked if he could show us where we were on our map. He pointed into the air about 3 inches "north" of the map. Great, just great. How the hell did we do that? Fortunately, no one pointed any fingers. We just turned around and headed back through the growing traffic and smog of downtown London. It took us 3 hours to get out of the city. 3 hours! I wondered how we were going to cover 14 countries in 5 and 1/2 months. Reality was starting to sink in. Not to mention the muscle ache, sore crotch (these padded pants aren't that great are they?), sweaty helmet head and downright exhaustion…

Once we got into the countryside it was a lot better. It was scorching hot and we all got burnt, but the scenery is so incredible! Red brick country houses and farms, beautiful old churches and ancient graveyards, and green, green, green.

We stopped in Hillingdon for lunch after 5 1/2 hours. We would've stopped sooner, but we couldn't find any place open on a Sunday. We were starved and dehydrated. The water is so unsatisfying – salty and dry. It leaves me feeling even thirstier.

One thing that was pretty cool was how people cheered us on when they saw us go by. We all wore our Larry shirts so they yelled out "Larry" as we passed, whistling and cheering. One girl hung out a car window with her thumb up in the air and yelled "Yo Larry!" That one, I think, is going to stick. We used it for the rest of the day. When we arrived at the youth hostel in Jordans, I was so relieved to peel myself off my bike. God, did I need a shower, and a massage, and a bed… It was closed. Closed! So we were directed another mile up the road (and they weren't kidding about the "up"). I could've cried. We were told there was a farm up there that had a small store where they sell eggs and milk and they might let us tent. They did thank god. I can't believe how sore I am. My whole body hurts, especially my neck, shoulders, and my right knee. My legs feel like Jello.

I'd looked forward to a shower all afternoon but no such luck. It was the old sink in the barn for the Larry Losers tonight. We gathered around in our underwear, actually happy to have even cold water to clean the sweat off our tired bodies. We got the giggles at the picture of ourselves standing in hay, pushing cobwebs aside, ignoring potent odors, sunburnt and smiling as we sponge bathed and got freeze-brain from washing our hair. We'd ridden our first 40 miles and felt the accomplishment under our exhaustion. It made for an enjoyable dinner and lots of laughs at our 3-hour tour of London.

April 30

OUCH!! Oh god.

May 1

Now we're in Oxford, home of the oldest English university and museum in the world, and birthplace of the amazing Stephen Hawking. We decided to take the day off for sightseeing and rest. Yesterday was brutally painful. I woke up stiff as a board and cranky as hell and didn't loosen up for several hours (in any way). I set a slow pace behind the others to give my hugely swollen knee a break and to be alone without worrying about anyone catching up. I think this'll be my position for the trip as I've realized I hate that feeling of someone being behind me. I spent the morning ranting to myself about everything. It was hot, the hills were getting longer, I was tired and sore, and I HATE the traffic. I ended up in the ditch twice from trucks coming by too close and too fast. It helps when they honk *as* they're passing you – just in case you weren't already having a heart attack… I hate breathing their smog and having to share the damn narrow roads with them. I had thoughts of hitchhiking, quitting, getting squashed, selling my bike, traveling by train, and killing Jamie for thinking up this nightmare in the first place.

We stopped in High Wycombe for lunch. Beans, fries, and toast for everyone and an ice pack for me. What's with the beans?

Maybe that's why we're constipated. Do beans do that? Could be the water. That water has to do something wicked. Jamie's been referring to us as "little rabbits" all week, due to the "pellet" phenomenon. When we were at the Tower of London, we went into an empty public washroom. I was taking a long time, so Jamie asked me if I was being a little rabbit. I said "Nooo, I'm being a biiiig rabbit." They laughed and then I carried on talking and making jokes. When I came out, they were gone and there were 3 nuns standing there looking at me. My so-called friends were outside laughing their heads off. "Well if it isn't the biiiig rabbit," Jamie says. Thanks guys. Thanks a heap.

The countryside really is gorgeous and I kept trying to enjoy it and remember why I wanted to cycle. I know it will eventually get easier but that seems so far off. Halfway through the afternoon I caught up to Jo, singing by herself on the road (she said I ruined her solo). We rode together, chatting about movies and stuff, which kept my mind off my frustrations. It helped a lot and my mood was much better when we arrived in Oxford. Jamie was here waiting for us. We decided to sleep at the hostel and enjoy the comfort of real beds. The building is gorgeous, old English architecture. There are 116 beds, showers (yeah!!), and lots of travelers to talk to.

At 6 am, a German girl's alarm went off, and it went and it went… until every single woman in the dorm was awake - except her (there are 9 sets of bunks in our room). Once shaken awake, she turned her clock off, rolled over and fell back to sleep. The rest of us got up. We were waay awake. No point in lying there.

After breakfast, Jo headed off to do some sightseeing while Jamie and I opted for a lazy row on the river. It was great - just what I needed. We took turns rowing into bushes and running aground… and took a couple pics of the "perm-ness monster" (You're welcome Larry… oh and thanks for the river slime; it goes well with my outfit). The architecture and gardens of Oxford are very beautiful. The university dates back to the 12th century and is made up of 39 colleges. Of course Jamie was more interested in the college boys than the buildings…

We picked up some groceries (and popsicles) and went back to the hostel, where we hung out in the backyard and played crib. Jamie won, but it was a fluke! Little so and so kept asking me if I wanted to concede half way through the game (and maybe I should have). Anyway it was fun. Jo came back when we were lying in our beds writing postcards. We cooked a nice pasta dinner and afterward Jamie and I took our tea outside, played another game of crib, and suffered Jamie's post-meal tribute to the chef. Jamie – "You cut". Me – "You just did" ha ha ha.

Later, we went in search of a laundromat, only to find it closed – so the next best thing – pub time! Got a good buzz on and checked the time at 5 to 11 – oh, oh, the hostel locks the door at 11. So we hopped in a taxi and arrived just in time to find it – locked. Awesome. My sore body wasn't going to be anywhere but in a bed. I'll huff and I'll puff… Fortunately, we just had to knock on the door and someone kindly let us in.

Jo was sleeping but she'd left a note on my pillow. It said, "Watch out for the top bunk. It might be bombs away." My top bunk had been empty the night before, but tonight it was occupied by a very large girl. After reading Jo's note I thought, "That's not very nice" and crawled under the covers. I looked up at the sagging bulge in the mattress above me and couldn't help but worry a little. I rolled over and tried to push it out of my mind. Jo, what a loser you are. I was just about asleep when the girl moved above me. The bed creaked and seemed to fold under her weight. The mattress seemed to hang just above my face, the shape of her body on the verge of crashing through. Jesus, the beds were lame. The frame seemed more fragile with every creak. This was all Jo's fault, so I decided she was toast! I plotted my revenge as I clung to the side of my bed, ready to bail out any minute.

May 2

I was up before anyone else – gee, I wonder why? We set our goal as Cheltenham, about 45 miles away. The first hour and a half was on a service road/path at the side of the highway. It was flat and out of the traffic, so I was happy and actually sang songs all the way (no one within torturing distance except for a few sheep but... did they say "baaaad"?). When I had to be on the highway again, I felt my energy instantly drop and the negative thoughts took over. When we stopped for lunch, I thought about it a lot. I feel so vulnerable at the side of the highway. The trucks scare me to death and there are tons of dead animals on the road, elevating my fear of being crunched.

By the time we hit the road again, I felt determined to overcome it. Six hours a day riding alone on the highway gives you lots of time to think. It made me realize why we fill our minds and lives with so many distractions – to avoid being alone with ourselves, our fears, etc. I found that I had a very distinct pattern of energy loss when traffic picked up. At one point, we had a whole lane marked off to ourselves and my energy burst from me... I cruised. When it ended and I was back on the highway, it dropped again. I thought about my fear and I decided I didn't want to die and it wouldn't be my time until I was ready. I chanted a mantra at the trucks: "I am the creator of my life". My energy increased and I picked up speed until I was really moving. The traffic seemed to thin out and the scenery was more beautiful.

A couple hours later, I caught up to Jamie and Jo. Jo said I was just a few minutes behind her. They looked hot and tired and Jamie said she didn't think the traffic had thinned at all. She told me later that she'd expected me to arrive cursing traffic and was surprised to see I was positive and smiling and saying, "Isn't this great?" I suggested we ride on to some place we could get a cold drink and rest. Along the way, we came upon a large truck carrying about 8 new cars. The cab of the truck and half the cars were engulfed in flames. The traffic was stopped quite far back, but Jamie just rode on through. Jo thought it might blow up and was hesitant to go near it. I suggested we push our bikes up the embankment and pass by along the top of the hill. Jo suggested we could make a dive for it if there was an explosion. What a drudge it was pushing our bikes and gear up that hill in the mid-afternoon sun! We managed to get by, but not without one small scream from Jo when something popped in the fire. We stopped at one point when there were a lot of pops. Jo quickly put her helmet on and said, "I'm going to dive now." We ran down the hill in a gale of giggles. What a loser.

We had intended to go to a hostel in Cleeve Hill just outside of Cheltenham. We'd already cycled uphill from town, having missed our turn, when we arrived at the foot of the very steep Cleeve Hill. We stood there, panting, the tiredness creeping quickly into our sore bodies. We noticed a camping sign that said one and a half miles and pointed downhill. Guess what? We went for it – and what an awesome downhill cruise it was... We arrived (in Woodmancote) at a gorgeous campground in a field with showers, laundry, and a pub/restaurant. Can't beat that! We set up our tents near a fence with sheep grazing only a few feet away. Jo had a tent of her own, but Jamie and I were sharing a tent we'd borrowed from a friend. Like sleeping with a lumberjack, so I came equipped with industrial strength earplugs and an "Okay, I've got to relax so I can fall asleep before she does" psych-myself-up kind of attitude.

We all had dinner in the restaurant after nice hot showers and tossing a load of laundry in. Jamie and I stayed up long after Jo, drinking wine and talking about death. Jamie had also spent a lot of her time on the road dealing with fear. I told her about "No Boundary" and how (if I understood Ken Wilber) it makes sense that we'd face fear as we "come into our bodies" again. He proposes that the body's vulnerability to pain, both physical and emotional, causes us to detach and identify with only our minds. The result being that we live in our heads and ride our bodies around like horses. Well, I definitely feel in touch with my body these days – my right knee, back, neck, shoulders, wrists, headache, constipation, allergies, sunburn, stinging nettles (so much for that shortcut)... No wonder I've been cranky.

I feel like I'm learning about myself, and I do feel the accomplishment at the end of the day. I've had some really good moments on the road. The sights and smells of the countryside (a lot better than our tent), the wind in my hair when I fly down those well earned hills (got to keep my mouth shut though – I nearly killed myself today when a bug hit the back of my throat and I jumped off my bike while it was still moving – GROSS!). I like being by myself on the road. It's hard when I'm frustrated because my mind seems to have the ability to make my bike weigh 2000 pounds, but when I'm happy and cruising... I feel so free. I love coming into these little towns too. The people are so nice, cheering us on, asking a zillion questions. It makes me feel good. Meeting the people. Isn't that what travel is all about? On our bikes, we really get the best of both – the sights and the people. We're not rushing by on a train, looking through a window. We're in the scenery. Seeing it, feeling it, breathing it.

It's easy to say this sitting here on this nice cushy chair; I hope I can remember it when I'm back on my not-so-cushy bike seat...

May 3

I woke up to the birds singing and the sun pelting down on the tent, a throbbing knee, and a dull ache in my lower back. I kept thinking I should open the door but just lay there in a comatose state. Jamie finally unzipped the door and let a cool breeze in so we could sleep a little longer. Thanks Larry. I got up about 8:30 and sat in the sun, writing and watching the sheep after washing up. I saw a bird land on a sheep's back and ride around while the sheep grazed, appearing not to notice. How cute! The bird paced back and forth, and even hopped onto the sheep's head for a while. I was looking away at one point and a sheep I hadn't noticed came close to the fence and let out a big "baaa". I jumped and let out a little cry of surprise. Jo giggled in her tent and said it had startled her too. A horse came up to the fence just after that so I dug out an apple and called the girls to come and see. He was gorgeous and loved our attention. A nice moment until we realized we were standing in those damn stinging nettles...

Today was a weird day. I ended up in a struggle with Jo over whether to stay another night or not. Communication is so tough sometimes. I have such a hard time feeling okay about wanting something different. I usually just go with the flow, but I feel less willing to do that recently and it makes me feel guilty. As I write this I feel myself pulling way deep inside, hiding, and just wanting to sleep. Somehow I know this trip is about it being totally okay to be me, not only when someone else agrees. It's okay for me to be different, to believe something different, want something different, and I don't have to defend it or explain it.

Jamie and I went to the pub after dinner for "one" drink and a game of crib, and it turned out to be a blast. The owner of the pub was a wonderful lady named Mary. She had two children and had run the pub with her husband until he passed away 6 years ago. When she spoke of her husband I could still see the grief in her eyes but she had a zest for life and seemed fairly content. She told us stories of hot air ballooning and asked us if we knew her niece who lived in America. "Where in America does she live?" we asked kindly (by now used to people not really comprehending the size of Canada).

"Rio" she said with sincerity.

"What's her name?"

"Katie McCallum."

"Does she have blonde hair?"

"No, red."

"No, I'm sorry I don't. How about you Jamie?"

"No, I don't know her either. Sorry."

Before long, the bar was closed and we were surrounded by the staff, drunk and full of stories. I was mesmerized by the manager, Norma, a fascinating woman full of information about history, the area, and more. She lived across the street in a 250-year-old cottage. She told us Woodmancote was where the Bishop of Cheltenham came to escape the plague when it was rampant in the city, how the beautiful yellow fields we were seeing was rape seed used for cooking oil (canola), and made us roar at how funny it was for them to see all the American movies about Robin Hood in which no one has a British accent. It was her accent that captivated me. I could've listened to her for days. We drank and laughed and yakked until 2 in the morning. After making promises we probably won't be able to keep and saying our good-byes, we stumbled to our tent and passed out.

May 4

Well, needless to say, Jamie and I slept in. Jo was gone by 7:30. Us at 11:30, and in rather poor shape I must admit. It was a quiet day, highlighted by food stops and ice cream remedies. We were headed to Christchurch campsite just before Monmouth. The climb into England's first National Forest Park, the Forest of Dean, was tough but well worth the view, even today. I had visions of my legs exploding, the mess on the highway, having to get a train pass, and the view from my first class compartment… Jo wasn't at the campsite (nor were most of the campers as they were glued to TV sets inside their trailers) but we called around and found her at the youth hostel in Monmouth. We made plans to pick her up in the morning, and had a very early night. Even snore bear wasn't going to keep me awake.

May 5

We were up and packing by 7:30. Picked up Jo and cycled to Crickhowell (Wales), birthplace of the man Mount Everest was named after (George). Supposedly, he never climbed Everest, but was a pioneer surveyor in Asia in the early 1800's. I think people like him are amazing. They set out from some little town like this one and crossed the world, exploring and mapping unknown places, facing unfathomable challenges and dangers. And I whine about the traffic and the hills…

We set up camp in a tiny, crowded site with gross "portaloo's" and pay showers (the kind that run out when you've got a head full of shampoo). After a good walk around town we ended up - can ya guess? - in a pub. Well, we are on holidays, we're working hard, we're tired, and it's a great place to meet people.

We talked a long while with some older men who bought us drinks, and asked a zillion questions about Canada, most of which we couldn't answer. Like "What's the population?" and hard stuff like that. One guy knew all the answers because he'd done a project on BC when he was a kid. Way to go Fred! Another Welsh guy said a word that had 52 letters in it. They wanted us to try and repeat it – yeah right! It was the name of a place in Wales. We had a good time with them and were feeling pretty good by the time they left. We took our drinks outside afterwards. It's cool how they all stand around outside the pub and drink. We met a group of army boys from Liverpool. They sounded like the Beatles and it was funny to listen to them. There was Pete, the oldest, probably late 30's, Neil 28, Jim 24 (who Jo liked and kept leaning on all night), and Andy who was shy and quiet. They're all part-time and voluntary, here for a week. We hadn't eaten dinner and were doing the slur and stagger something fierce. God that cider on tap is wicked, wicked (but delicious) stuff.

I called Donna from the pay phone inside. It was about 3 p.m. Canada time. I don't remember what we talked about except that when one of the Liverpool guys went by on his way to the bathroom, I grabbed him and said to Donna, "Talk to this guy, he sounds like a Beatle." Poor guy. I was homesick when I got off the phone and didn't mind that it was time to go. Oh yeah, at one point Jo had some guy on the opposite side of the bar saying, "Yo Larry" to get my attention. She was hiding behind him as if I wouldn't notice that blonde bob and weave stuck to his back. Then, she got us kicked out when a waiter dropped a glass after being hit by one of several coasters she was winging across the bar at me.

On the way back to the campsite, Jamie teased Jo about "young studmuffin Jim" and "boinkarama". How old are we? Jo found her tent all caved in and after a lame and unsuccessful attempt to set it back up, she gave up and crawled in. Seconds later, she did the loudest fart, I swear, that I have ever heard in my life. Jamie and I collapsed in laughter and literally rolled on the ground, tears streaming from our eyes. (Of course by the next day, there had been shouting in the streets, children crying out in their sleep, and a national alarm). Jamie and I tried to pull ourselves together to go visit a group of people standing nearby but couldn't stop laughing and were SURE they'd heard old foghorn too. We gave up and sat outside our tent smoking for a while. Before crashing, we inhaled Jamie's cookies (which I might have forgotten if I hadn't found chocolate cookie crumbs floating in my contact lens case this morning).

Quote of the day: Jo: "I want to kiss the blimey stone".

May 6

We walked to a store for chocolate today. We said we'd each get a different kind and share a taste. Jo spent over 30 minutes picking out her bar, determined to get the best one. Jamie and I were outside waiting when she came out, grinning, bar in hand. We each handed her a piece of ours and before trying her own she handed it to us. "Don't tell me if my chocolate bar's gross," she said as we bit into it. "How is it?" she asked with anticipation. We handed it back, smiled, and walked away…

May 7

I dreamt I was sick from the "Smash" insty potatoes (what a shocker).

We only rode about 6 miles today and then caught the train to Swansea (still Wales). When we arrived in Swansea, we found out that there are only two trains a day going to Fishguard (where we'll catch a ferry to Rosslare, Ireland), and we'd missed the first one. That left us with the 11:15 p.m., arriving in Fishguard at 1:30 am. And that meant we had to choose between a night in Fishguard or catching the 3:15 am ferry, arriving in Rosslare at 6:45 am. Ouch! We decided to go for the sleepless night and bought our tickets. So we had 9 hours to kill in cold and windy Swansea. Because the weather was bad and we were tired, we decided to hang out in a pub. We didn't want to drink, but in pubs you can hang around for hours, play cards, write in journals, etc.

Before we did that though we grabbed some disgusting fish and chips (it's not our day) and hung out on the lawn of the local castle for a couple hours. Jamie entertained us with her rendition of "Bean Band on the Run" by "Fartley Crue", complete with sound effects, which Jo joined in for. I ask again, "How old are we?" Jo also did her impression of the scary guy from "Black Christmas" (the eye peeking through the crack in the door). We had a serious discussion about all our favourite Bugs Bunny cartoons and Jo reminded us of that old cartoon with the hobo flea going after the dog – "♫ There's food around the corner, food around the corner, food around the corner for meeee ♫".

Later, in the pub, we met two guys who insisted on joining our card game. They seemed okay at first but one in particular got weirder by the minute. He paid a lot of attention to me from the beginning, though we were sure they were gay (turned out to be a gay bar). Before I knew it, he was insulting me and criticizing me. He said things like, "I'm so disappointed in you Riley, you're not like I thought", etc. He actually became angry and abusive about it. I ignored him and moved away, and just focused on having a good time with the Larrys. He kept pushing it though and I finally just said, "Look Herbert, I feel good about who I am and I don't care what you think." He stayed angry and went on to criticize us for not staying in Swansea and learning the history, etc. I felt like he was trying to control me, not just judging, but trying to manipulate through his judgement. It was easy to see it as his stuff, and that I had a choice to let it affect me or not. So I just kept having fun with the girls.

Jo kept trying to scare me in the bathroom (and usually succeeded), which is also the place for the quote of the day: Jo was standing sideways in front of the mirror and she said, "This is how thin I want my thighs to be." I looked and said, "Can you suck in your thighs?" (failing to see that she was marking part off with her hand). We howled all the way back to the table. Separately, however, as Jo wouldn't be seen with me after that comment... We chair surfed, had a tickle fight, and tried to buy a joint from a group of women sitting beside us who, on second look, were probably a bad guess. Oh well, we certainly didn't need it. So we blew that popsicle stand, slightly different than we'd entered, and caught our train.

It was a terrible night, as the alcohol wore off and the hours passed painfully slow until we could board the ferry at 2:30 am. Once aboard, I found a piece of floor to sleep for a few hours before dragging myself to my feet at 6 am to clean up and get some tea. My first sunrise over the Atlantic... We docked at 7, but had to hang around the terminal until the hostel opened at 9.

There was no one around when we got to the hostel, just a sign that said registration was at 5:30 pm and you had to be out by 10 am. AND, there were no showers or hot water due to construction! We settled for a nearby B&B, where we happily climbed into 3 cushy beds at 10 am for a much needed nap. Did I say "cushy" beds? That's an understatement. They were soooo comfortable, but they were so old that they drooped in the middle - big time! So much so, in fact, that when I woke up at 3:30, I thought Jamie had already left. Her blankets lay flat over her bed, like it was empty. When she suddenly sat up while Jo and I were chatting, she startled the hell out of us! While I bathed to go out for dinner, I remembered the feeling of my dreams. I don't know what they were but I had a strong, weird feeling and I kept thinking of Herbert in Swansea. Seems I wasn't unaffected by his judgement after all. Perhaps the universe was just giving me another opportunity to choose to feel good about myself no matter what anyone else thinks.

We headed out to eat feeling a lot better than before, and even managed a few choruses of "There's food around the corner". It didn't take long to discover that Rosslare has no main street and only 3 restaurants, which are in the hotels. After dinner we sat in the lounge, drinking tea and writing in our journals. It's pretty here, overlooking the harbour. I can see part of England and the Irish coastline looks beautiful, although it's very cold and cloudy now. I saw a few drops of rain. Eighty-eight miles to Dublin, so two days riding and we'll be there.

May 9

Wow, did I ever have a bizarre dream last night. I had arrived home from my trip and was greeted by Mom and Leanne. I was really confused because I only remembered my trip up until last night and I didn't know why I was home already. I asked Leanne how long I'd been gone and she said 5 months. I tried to remember more of the trip, but couldn't. Not Greece or Egypt. Not Turkey. I didn't tell anyone. They were happy to see me and it seemed like I'd been gone a long time but god, what happened and why didn't I remember? I joined Mom in the kitchen and a neighbour was there and they were talking to me and someone said something about my marriage. I was shocked. I said, "What?" "Did I get married?" They said, "Yeah, you got married in Portugal." I tried to remember, but drew a complete blank. I woke up to a knock at the door at 8:15.

Up and packing slowly, grouchy. I joined Jo and Jamie for breakfast with the elderly woman who ran the B&B. She was very sweet. I told them all about my dream and they teased me that maybe I'd meet someone along the way. Ya right. So many people had said that when I left. It couldn't possibly happen that often yet when people find out you're going to travel around Europe, practically the first thing they say is, "Maybe you'll meet someone." Diehard romantics I guess.

It was a great day for riding, cool, and it even rained a bit. Got out the gortex for the first time. My energy level was high and the road fairly flat and quiet. That helps! Gorgeous green farmland, thatched cottages, and Barnaby the sheepdog highlighted the day. Stopped at a B&B in Gorey for the night and whipped up a big yummy batch of Ratatouille for dinner.

May 10

Just when I thought it couldn't get any worse than sleeping next to Frankensnore, we're crammed into a tiny little bed that sinks in the middle. If we weren't colliding, then my bum was hanging off the edge thanks to a certain bed HOG. My lower back was killing me and I was the grouchiest f'n thing anybody'd ever seen when the night from hell was finally over.

At breakfast, we were a little ticked off when they brought us porridge and toast – cuz we knew that the permanent guests (workers from out of town) had been served bacon and eggs just before us. We whined and complained to each other about the crappy breakfast, filling up for our morning ride. About the time we'd pretty much had our fill, they brought out our breakfast main course – huge plates of eggs, potatoes, sausages, and bacon. We felt foolish and sick. Good thing we hadn't said anything. So we laughed at each other as we crammed it down, and took turns doing the restaurant scene from The Meaning of Life ("Just a wafer thin mint?"). A Larry way to start the day...

I was in a foul mood and couldn't help feeling guilty about it. I didn't aim it at anyone, but there was no way I could hide it. Jamie was pissed at me. Why do I feel so responsible for her experience? I can't even allow myself to be grumpy without beating the hell out of myself for how it affects others. I'm realizing more and more how guilt affects my life, my actions, my self-esteem. Why do I think I have to be so goddamned perfect? Truth is, if Jamie doesn't like my mood, that's her problem and up to her to sort out. I'm not doing anything to her, and she's not even with me all day. My mood is mine. Her anger is her problem. Oh this is exhausting, especially today.

I was ready to hand over the tent poles at one point and tell them I'd meet them in Dublin, but I met up with Jo on the road and she cheered me up a bit playing 20 questions for movie stars. By the time we met Jamie in Arklow, I'd decided I really wanted to go to Glendalough (Valley of Two Lakes) too. I read that it is one of the most important sites of monastic ruins in Ireland.

It turned out to be a beautiful ride. No houses for long periods of time, no cars, just me and the trees and the sound my bike makes on the road. Openings to views of mountains, valleys, streams, and sprays of pretty blue, violet, and yellow flowers. By the time I arrived at Laragh, I was tired but I felt really good. My mood had lifted. Jamie's bike was parked in front of the pub, one of the few buildings in this tiny mountain town. I wondered where Jo's bike was. Glendalough was just around the corner so I figured she was getting settled. Jamie was having a beer with an Australian girl named Jenny, a Californian named Tim, and Tom, an Irishman who'd picked them up hitchhiking. I was greeted warmly by big grins. Hopped on a bar stool and ordered a spritzer. Jamie hadn't seen Jo and it was 4:30. I wondered where I'd passed her.

Jenny and Tim were traveling together for a while. He'd just finished a year at Oxford and Jenny was a teacher, who'd just finished her degree – and was doing a 3-year tour of the world! Both really nice people, and Tom was great. He loved traveling himself and said he took any chances he could to meet travelers, help out if he could, and hear all about their travels. Keeps his life interesting he said. We had lots of laughs as we swapped stories of our experiences so far.

At 6:30, Jo finally rolled in. She'd taken a wrong turn and ended up lost on logging roads in the mountains. She was very tired (2 hours more cycling than us) and very upset. She told me later that she took a picture of herself crying in frustration at the side of the road. She figured it was a part of her trip she should capture on film. Poor Larry... She went down to the hostel we'd apparently passed on the way up. Jenny, Tim, and Tom left shortly after.

Jamie and I kept on drinking and soon we were very drunk. After that long climb up into the mountains, all we'd had was a side of fries. Not enough to soak up the booze that was going down like water. It wasn't long before we were arguing about me inflicting my mood on her. I said that I'd tried really hard not to "inflict" it. I hadn't yelled at her or grumbled or criticized. I'd just been quiet and not cheerful. Shouldn't I be able to feel how I feel? I couldn't help that I was in a bad mood. I asked her why she needed me to be in a good mood all the time. I suggested that she ask herself what was really bothering her. She hadn't even seen me all day and I was in a great mood when I arrived – until she started bitching at me. She didn't appreciate that and before long it was, "Oh you're always trying to be so enlightened." Then about how I contradict myself all the time, and I don't live what I preach. She was right about that part. I talk about making healthy choices for our bodies and our minds (loving ourselves), but I'm not taking very good care of myself. I'm drinking too much, smoking, and always hammering away at myself for my imperfections. I'm always striving for acceptance. I can't handle criticism in any form, or people being angry at me – and especially being wrongly accused. I defend and explain myself constantly. Why am I so hard on myself? Where does it come from? Why can't I just accept myself for who I am?

Jamie was very angry with me and it hurt. Somehow we changed the subject and moved to a table. We chatted with some Irish boys: Austin (25) and 3 boys (15-16) he'd taken fishing. Dean (we signed the cast on his arm), Neville (drew a map so we could go to a BBQ at his house the next day), and Jake (beautiful curly hair, blushing face, and quiet – not one word). They were all nice and it was fun to talk to them but we had to wonder about Austin with these under-agers in the pub, getting them beer and talking about how their parents don't trust him. They left about 10 because it was a school night. After they left was extremely blurry (a shift from fairly blurry). Jamie and I talked about her brother's suicide and her tendency to push family and friends away. She cried, I comforted her, and we exchanged I-love-you-buddys. She would only let herself get close to people for so long. She can't handle people counting on her and seems to purposely let them down. With most friends she comes on like an explosion, jumping in with both feet, changing the other person's life forever. But eventually, she fades out, disappointing them time and time again until they finally give up. She stands people up on dinner invites, forgets birthdays, disappears for months on end… She's fooled around on most of her lovers. Avoids her family like the plague. Even the friends that love her most finally let her go. She doesn't hold up her end. It seems any kind of commitment scares the hell out of her. I think losing her brother, especially to suicide, made it almost impossible for Jamie to relax into a deep relationship with anyone. Of course she has other issues that started before that tragedy. Issues of self-esteem like me, which is perhaps why she pushes me so hard sometimes.

Then we were fighting again, and it went on for a while. Stuff about how she has to wait for us, and whining about hills, and being wimps... I remember it ended with her saying I copied her by buying red suspenders for my riding tights and it pissed her off. She was spitting mad. I reminded her that she'd told us to get suspenders and so what if I picked red ones too? They only had two colors to choose from! I ended up getting really mad and raving about how I wanted to be just like her, "Yeah, that's it." I stood up and said I didn't have to listen to her BS and she should travel with someone else.

She followed me out the door and demanded the tent poles, so I tossed them at her and got my bike ready. I was so drunk I had tunnel vision. I heard a man's voice but didn't see him (Jamie told me later that he told us not to fight and not to ride our bikes – god, I wonder how loud we were). I rode about 30 yards and stopped dead. It was pitch black. I mean "can't-see-your-hand-in-front-of-your-face-Jesus-are-my-eyes-closed pitch black". I couldn't see a thing. Not a damn thing. I also didn't have a clue where the hostel was. I started laughing my head off and calling, "Yo Larry" into the dark.

Jamie rode up laughing and we hugged and laughed together. She guided the way with her flashlight in her teeth. I could hardly hold up my bike. I couldn't figure out how she could ride so steady when I was this staggering, swerving mess all over the road. Jamie called out, "Pull over, there's a car coming and you're on the wrong side." There's a side? I tried to pull over and went flying sideways off my bike, landing upside down in a ditch. Thank god I was wearing a helmet, and thank god the ditch was dry. I was upside down, laughing and couldn't move. Jamie pulled me out and we laid in a heap at the side of the road, howling. I decided to push my bike from there. We made it to the hostel, put up our tent, pigged out on chips and chocolate, smoked, and passed out.

May 11

Woke up with yet another wicked hangover, and pangs of humiliation sneaking into my throbbing mind. Why am I doing this?

Am I going to drink my way around Europe? Is this a sightseeing tour or a pub crawl? I couldn't help but laugh with Jamie about the ditch incident, but I was embarrassed to go into town and be recognized as the drunken idiot who'd been fighting in the bar the night before. "Hey, there's one of them now!" Jo dragged me in for tea and scones anyway, so I kept my head down and tried not to look anyone in the eye.

There I go giving a hoot again what people think but I guess it's my feelings about drinking so much. I have to slow down. I can't keep my head clear, and I feel like I'm missing so much. Partying is fun, sure, but I can do that at home – and do I have to do it every second night? I guess I feel worse about it when the crap comes out like with me and Jamie last night. It doesn't seem like we're drinking for fun when all that hits the fan. Drinking often makes me feel guilty, or maybe ashamed is the word, because somehow I know I'm trying to accomplish something through it. Like empowerment. Or hiding. I don't know. Who can think when it feels like someone sucked your brain out your nose? But I'm going to smarten up and start paying more attention to what I'm learning – or supposed to be learning…

It's a pretty area. The hostel is an old stone mill. Really cool idea, but too cold inside for me. I was happy to be staying in a tent. An American woman who lives in Germany told Jo and I the history of St. Kevin's Kitchen, a place nearby in the woods. We listened intently over vegetable soup as she told of St. Kevin, a man who'd gone there to be a monk and escape the world. Legend has it that he was followed there by a beautiful, blue-eyed woman who he killed, throwing her from the tower to the rocks below. She said the legend is told in a poem by Thomas Moore called, "By that Lake Whose Gloomy Shore".

Jamie and I walked there after an early dinner, led by two dogs from the hostel who ran ahead to guide us the minute we set foot on the trail. I hadn't told Jamie about the history, but filled her in quickly when she started complaining of an uneasy and eerie feeling as we walked around the ruins. It was disquieting, even in the bright sunshine. Silent, yet it seemed to whisper the past in our ears. Remnants of buildings. Mysterious tombstones. A beautiful blue-eyed woman. A tormented man. Anguish. Regret. We left totally spooked and hurried back to the hostel as the sun disappeared behind the mountain.

May 12

I had a scary dream. I was in a huge house. I had a little sister (about three), who I loved dearly. Friends were going to watch her while Mom & Dad were away and I was going to stay too. I was aware of a secret room way down below the house. A safe place. I also had a teenage sister who was having a party. I told her to clear everyone out. I didn't trust some of the people there. I picked up a bag someone had dropped for someone else and it was full of pot and money. They spotted me with it and I knew I was in danger. I went through the crowd. A man was following me. I knew if I could get to the secret room I'd be safe. I went through doors and crawled on floors because he was outside following through the windows. I didn't want him to find out about the room. Down, down, and more and more scared. So aware of him. I made it to the room, which had no windows, breathless, listening for him, and all of a sudden the power went out and I was in the pitch black. I knew he'd cut it. I was terrified. I woke up sweating.

basement (the safe place) = the unconscious?

the scary guy = fear

pitch black (like the other night) = can't see where I am?

What am I afraid of? What do I want to hide from?
It was a boring day on the road to Dublin, although Jo and I had a great two-hour conversation over lunch – about homesickness, friendships, lifestyles, etc. We rode the last 20 miles together after that, playing 20 questions and making good time. It was fun and made up for the lack of scenery and the cold dreary day.

May 13

Wow, what a great sleep I had. Nice comfy beds, and it's a really nice hostel (Kinlay House). It was nice to arrive last night to hot showers, clean beds, and laundry after a few nights of camping and that terrible sleep I had in Gorey. We took it easy last night, in bed early after enjoying a great dinner (Mediterranean) and sharing a big banana split with Jo (I'm sure she ate more than her half). I had an interesting dream. I was standing in a big circle of people. They said we had to find our light but I didn't know how. A friend showed me by flicking my thumb until a radiant light glowed from it. I had to stand in the middle of the circle with my thumb over my third eye (so light shone out like a flashlight). They went round and round me, and someone said I had to go around until I went somewhere. In my dream, I fell asleep and then woke up feeling like a kid – confused and upset, feeling I'd failed because I didn't get there. A friend was gentle and reassuring. Then I really woke up.

Today we went to "Paddy Slattery's, an Irish pub. It was "grand" as they say here in Dublin. We went there to hear some live music and were we ever glad we did. Guitars, fiddles, violins, mandolins, and a weird drum thing for a foot-tapping, Irish jig type jam. A merry time was had by all (it was packed). Irish people are so fun! We also had some good laughs over a comment in Let's Go Europe that referred to Vienna as the spy capital of the world. We imagined the smoky interrogation rooms and swinging lights – "My name is Larry and my rank is loser".

I called home tonight for Mother's Day and everyone was there waiting to talk to me. It was good to hear all their voices but so brief, in order to get through everyone. Little Jessica wanted to know how the doggie was that peed on my sweater… Her mother suggested I call sober next time and not bother putting drunk Beatles on the phone; she couldn't understand a word of it anyway. Yeah, whatever. Who invited you to this call?

I feel a little homesick now. I guess travel helps us not only appreciate other places and other peoples but also, our own family and friends. A bit of a surprise seeing as I could hardly wait to get out of there. I've even thought of not going back for a couple years if I can get a job or live on a Kibbutz. It's the weirdest thing, but somehow I feel like I can't be truly happy at home. I feel stuck, kind of trapped, but I don't know why.

May 14

Today we split up. Jo caught a ferry to go visit her relatives in Liverpool, while Jamie and I went through Belfast to get a ferry to Scotland – to visit her relatives. We don't have time to do it all if we're going to meet Jo's friends in Amsterdam by June 1. So we made plans with Jo to meet her in Edinburgh and carry on from there.

Jamie and I had a great day on the trains. The scenery between Dublin and Belfast, and from Stranraer to Clydebank in Scotland was fantastic. Green and more green. Lots of fir trees in Scotland, reminded us of home. Not that we forgot for a minute that we were in another new country as we giggled, "We're in Scotland" back and forth like kids. Jamie was really nervous about calling her relatives. Although her mom had written a letter telling them we were coming, Jamie had never met them before. She felt awkward about asking them if we could stay. When she phoned, she relaxed a little as her 81-year-old great auntie Emma assured her that they were expecting us and "of course" we were staying with her.

We were greeted at the door by auntie Emma, a plump woman with a cute little voice. Inside, we were introduced to Jamie's Uncle Don and Aunt Marion. They were all nice and welcoming, but the first half hour was a little tense. Older people, quiet house, manners – all the stuff that makes Jamie uptight. I couldn't help but chuckle to myself at her attempt to be polite and proper. She seemed like she had something stuck up her butt. She had such a weird expression on her face, stiff as a board, squeaky little voice. I soaked it all in so I could bug the hell out of her later.

Not long after Jamie's 19-year-old babe of a cousin Donny showed up, I nearly lost it all together. Jamie was sitting on the couch between gorgeous Donny and Aunt Marion, trying to be polite and make conversation (even the way she held her little sandwich on her napkin was too funny) – when I noticed that her fly was wide open and I mean "wide". It made such a funny picture with her trying to be proper that I nearly choked. I had to leave the room. I went into the kitchen and drank some water, trying to stifle my laughter, but every time I thought of going back in there and seeing her again I'd break. I went in and out of the bathroom 3 or 4 times. I tried cold water on my face, thinking sad thoughts, everything. I'd get to the doorway of the living room and lose it in hysterical giggling. I wanted to just roll on the floor and ba ha ha. I was gone so long someone asked if I was okay.

I finally had to hold it together and go back in. It took everything I had. I wouldn't look at her. I couldn't look at her. The only seat available was directly across from her. I sat down, noticed it was still open, and left the room. When I tried again after a few minutes, Jamie was standing at the table getting a sandwich with her back to everyone. She said, "What's with you?" so I whispered "Your fly." She looked down, said "Oh God", and I broke. I had to cover my mouth and leave the room again … people eyeing me suspiciously now. I hope they didn't think I was spitting their food in the toilet.

May 15

I seem to have developed a problem from the toilet paper. Well *they* call it toilet paper, *I* call it something you'd wrap sandwiches in. Thin, wax paper, that's what it is. I guess absorbency hasn't been invented here yet. We could make millions!

This was a vewy interesting day. Seems we've discovered a family secret. We started the day doing the "Aunt Emma shuffle", in and out of the alternating burning hot or freezing cold, zero-pressure, shower from hell. Ham and butter sanny's with tea and then cookies and tea with Donny's sister, wee Marion, when she arrived with her daughter Pamela at 11:30.

Marion took us to Jamie's great uncle Mac's. On the way, we asked her how her dad, Don, was related. When Jamie asked Auntie Emma earlier this morning if Don was Mac's son, she said yes, that he was Jamie's mom's cousin. Marion smiled strangely and said he was Granny McFarlane's (Jamie's great grandma). That didn't make sense because then he'd be Emma, Mac, and Jamie's grandma's brother – and why wouldn't Emma have just told us that? Besides he's a lot younger than them. So it was Watson and Holmes on the case after that, a.k.a. Larry and Larry, super sleuths extraordinaire. We exchanged knowing glances and fancy eyebrow manoeuvres.

Mac was a tall, shy man living in a trailer park. He offered us tea and more cookies (this is my kinda town). He has a big picture of Jamie's mom and himself on the wall and several smaller ones about the room. Funny, no pictures of Don anywhere. You'd think if Don was his brother or son...

After that, we did some sightseeing – a rainy but scenic drive up the coast to Largs, a wet walk up the beach, and some interesting tips from 3-year-old Pamela, "Crabs bite yer toes off and jellyfish sting ya." On the way back, she taught us hand aerobics in the car, "Up and down… Now, from the beginning…and you practice at home." Too cute! I wish I could capture her accent on paper. I love it when she says "wee". "Oh look at that wee boy", or "that wee house". The Scottish seem like such wonderful people. Even aside from Jamie's relatives, people seem so friendly and kind. The language is a joy to listen to (and sometimes decipher), and seems so gentle in its expressions and tone. Too bad my ancestors left so long ago. I would love to have some relatives here.

Before going back to Emma's, Marion ran us by her place to meet her husband Patrick. What a cutie pie! He looks like Robbie from the old 60's sitcom "My 3 Sons". Tea and you'll never guess… more cookies!

We had a nice dinner with Emma. She's a very sweet woman and although determined to avoid talking about Don, she told us all kinds of things about Jamie's family history and her own life with her hubby Hugh, who she's still mourning. They ran a hotel for 14 years. She's very racist, like many of the people we met in England, yet seems to have such a kind heart. It's really hard to understand the attitudes we've encountered here regarding other cultures, particularly Asian and African. I know racism exists in Canada – I overhear people's ridiculous jokes and comments. But it seems less. Maybe in Canada people just hide it more? Here, people come right out and say it. I really don't understand. Why is it so hard for people to accept differences? How can people say that they believe in a god, yet deny that every living thing on this planet must be part of that god? I guess I'm prejudiced against people who are racist. They sure piss me off.

Young Donny and Patrick picked us up for a night on the town. Then, we picked up Donny's girlfriend.

"Drats," says Jamie.

"He's your cousin," says Riley.

"Incest is best," says Jamie.

We did some pub hopping and were eventually joined by Marion, who'd been out with some buddies. Before she got there, I listened admiringly to her husband talk about environmental issues, but once she arrived we were "on the case" again. It didn't take much to get it out of her, no need for the crow bar or water torture. One drink, and she was putty in our hands. Turns out Don senior is Jamie's mom's half brother, the illegitimate son of Jamie's grandma. He was born before grandma married grandpa (different man), and adopted and raised by Granny McFarlane, his grandmother. When Jamie's grandma finally married and moved to England, where she had Jamie's mom and Gordon (Uncle "eyebrows"), Don was left behind. Jamie couldn't believe her mom had never told her that she had another brother. Bizarre. She couldn't wait to get home and find out why.

"Maybe she didn't want to justify your sleazy behavior" I said, smoking on Emma's window sill at 3 am, just before a pillow slammed into my head.

"Hey it's not me who wants to add incest to the family repertoire."

May 16

A quiet day today. Took Auntie Emma and her friend Mrs. Russell out for lunch. They're so formal with each other, like those cute little cartoon mice on TV. "Would you like some tea Mrs. Russell?" "Why yes, Mrs. McCarthy, some tea would be quite nice thank you".

Jamie called Mrs. Russell "Tootsie" under her breath when she came in. I nearly choked. A striking resemblance, minus the 5 o'clock shadow.

"Tea and cookies x 4, mmm," says Riley.

"Donny, fresh out of the bath, mmm," says Jamie.

May 17

Time to leave Clydebank and all the charming people we've met here. We hit the road after teary farewells, all loaded up with Scottish sausage, meat pies, and blood pudding. Can I trade it in for a few of those cookies?

An easy cycle to Loch Lomond, and some much-needed alone time. We met at the hostel, a gorgeous old castle we heard about from a traveler in Glendalough. Ditched the blood pudding upon arrival (a grateful staff member), and headed out for some real food. A good day, finished off with a good chat about relationships and sex. Jamie misses her boyfriend.

May 18

Another good day on the road – except for a head wind and those goddamned midgies. I swear I flicked 30 or 40 of them off me every 5 minutes. But, the scenery is pleasant and we had a delicious picnic under a tree along the way: avocado, cheese, onion, tomato, brown bread, and even mayo. Just like home. The sun was warm and soothing, restoring the energy I'd lost to the wind.

We were tired and sore when we arrived in Stirling; only to find out we had to ride to the highest point in the city. The hostel is like a small castle. When I went to pay for my bed, I realized I left my money belt under my pillow at the hostel in Loch Lomond. I freaked. Everything is in it. I called the hostel and they'd found it so I arranged for a courier to take it to Edinburgh tomorrow. I'm so pissed off at myself. What a waste of money!

We checked out the medieval Stirling castle, where Mary Queen of Scots was crowned. "Mary was a bad-ass," Jamie says, strutting a little in her Scottish heritage pride, "Did you know one of her three husbands was her first cousin?"

"Aside from being your cousin, Donny has a girlfriend and he's just a pup," I reminded her.

"Mary's cousin was younger than her. Besides, young flesh keeps us fresh," Jamie declared mischievously.

"Did you know that Mary was only 44 when she was executed for plotting to assassinate Elizabeth?" I asked, trying to change the subject.

"Too bad. We're supposed to hit our sexual peak in our 40's. Just think of the fun she probably had with those hot young courtiers," Jamie replied, not to be deterred from the ancestral justification of her lecherous ways.

"I read that the executioner dropped Mary's head because he didn't know she was wearing a wig to cover her short grey hair," I announced.

Jamie stopped and turned around to look at me.

"And it rolled across the floor," I added.

Jamie just smiled and walked away. Apparently I'd won the round.

When we went to our room at curfew, we discovered a school group was surrounding us – noisy, screeching kids. We asked to move and they told us to grab any room we wanted. We went way down into the depths of the castle, away from everyone and found a quiet room. Quiet isn't actually the best word to describe this room. Silent? Still? Dead? Don't get carried away now Larry. It's just a room. But it's so cold. We have lots of blankets though. I'm starting to warm up. Jamie didn't last long in her journal; she's snoring major already. Time to sleep. If possible.

May 19

Last night, just after I turned out the lights, Jamie yelled out in her sleep, "You guys, she's coming.... she's here!" I nearly jumped out of my skin. Totally spooked I lay awake for ages, only my eyes peaking out from under the covers, wondering, "Who's here?" Doo – doo, doo – doo.

Cycling into Edinburgh was gross – horrendous traffic and crowds, choking on exhaust... Found a cool youth hostel though, got my money belt (♪ oh what a relief it is ♪), and headed out to see the sights. Off the bike, it was much easier to take.

We ended the day in a hall someone told us about with a folk rock band. Packed solid, but a cultural experience I believe. Another drunk argument with Jamie – this time because I got heavy and self-deprecating. I ended up crying and feeling extremely pathetic. The familiar body-chemistry of shame and self-loathing bubbled up from there. These moments certainly don't help my self-esteem, that's for sure. I feel even worse in the morning.

It's been eight years since I decided that life is the only option. How long do I have to keep choosing? How long do I have to keep trying to think positively and focus on what I'm grateful for? I'm in Europe for Pete's sake, living a dream – a dream I worked hard for. And I'm having fun! Why did the mire follow me here? Jamie reminded me of that Hemmingway quote, "You can't get away from yourself by moving from one place to another." Thank you oh wise one...

When we got back to the hostel we found that Larry #1 had checked into our room. She was asleep so we snuck in and crashed.

May 20

Up to rustling. Happy to see Jo. Had fun looking at her pics over breakfast and lots n' lots of tea. Jamie and I decided not to hang around in Edinburgh. We wanted to do some more cycling and camping, spend some time around Cambridge and be able to stay with Jamie's mom's best friend in Essex before having to get to Amsterdam for the 1st. So we parted again, Jamie and I jumping on a train bound for Nottingham. We intended to meet Robin 'ood and his band of merry men.

Well we didn't meet any heroes but some very helpful locals. We got lost, you see, and we went from one helpful person to yet another helpful person. No hostels to start with, so directed to a B & B three miles up the road. Too expensive, so directed to a place to camp. No one there, so two sweet young boys on motorbikes tried to help us. They led us here and there, and here again, and finally directed us to a ranger in the forest. He was on holiday. The caretaker said no camping but directed us to a field up the road. It was getting dark fast, and there was a really cold wind. We finally found the field after hauling our bikes under a barbed wire fence, and doing some off road trail riding. It was lumpy but deserted and I just wanted to get out of the wind. I warmed up a little when we had to chase the tent across the field. Should have put some weight in it right away I guess.

May 21

Slept pretty good considering. A little shifting around the bumps and the wind blew hard all night. It was like sleeping in a kite.

A tough day today, some of our biggest hills yet, and with that damn headwind. I almost cried in frustration a few times. Finally arrived at the campsite just outside of Langdon. Set up, shared a bottle of wine and played crib while ratatouille cooked. Ate in 10 minutes flat, tomato moustaches and happy grins.

A much needed hot shower, after cycling all day in the clothes we'd slept in. Need to do laundry something fierce. My shower went cold and I was left naked in the freezing stall waiting for none other than Larry hot water boag, to finish next door. When it came back on, I savoured every second, letting the heat work at my sore muscles. Forty-five miles of hills to look forward to tomorrow, if we don't find camping before Huntingdon.

It crossed my mind that fighting the headwind could represent the struggle within myself – between the part of me that wants to love myself and give myself a break, and the part of me that seems to hate me.

May 22

Decided to take the train to Cambridge from Stamford and stay a day. Two miles into Langham for cream tea – a nice healthy breakfast of scones, jam, and whipped cream, but didn't really wake up until about half way through the 11-mile ride to Stamford. I must say my pace is picking up – my legs must be getting stronger. We both fell asleep on the train and were startled awake by the conductor announcing Cambridge station. Stumbled sleepily out of the train, bikes dragging. We rode into Cambridge where I went to the American Express office while Jamie went to call Todd. She was gone a long time and when she finally came back, she was crying. It didn't seem like just an "I miss him" cry, but I didn't ask. It was pretty clear that she wasn't ready to talk about it.

We rode through Cambridge, which is wonderful. The architecture, quaint little shops, and bicycles made me smile and I loved it instantly. The campsite was past the city so we rode on through, knowing we'd have time to come back and explore. Just outside of town, there were large pylons on the grass on the side of the road, and when I rode by one, it lifted up and a guy was grinning at me. He was standing in a hole up to his shoulders so the pylon completely covered him. It was hilarious.

Jamie was riding hard so I knew she was really upset, and whenever she waited for me I could see she'd been crying more. I wondered if Todd had broken up with her, but I couldn't imagine it. They seemed to adore each other. Todd was probably the first guy in ages (or ever) that Jamie hadn't fooled around on.

We rode 10 miles instead of the 3 to the campsite, because we missed our turn. Finally arrived and it was nice – showers, laundry (everyone say "hallelujah" now), a store, and Jamie got directions to a pub (I had a feeling she'd be needing a drink). She went straight away, no shower, no laundry. I really didn't want to go before showering, but I knew she was upset so I asked her if she wanted me to go with her. She said she needed to be alone for a while but to meet her when my laundry was done.

When I got to the pub, she handed me a letter she'd written to Todd. Apparently, he'd told her he'd gone camping with some of our friends and Kirsten and Amber's tent had a leak so they'd slept in the van with him, one on either side. Well Jamie was furious, deeply hurt, and ready to let Todd go. Nothing had happened, but she was extremely jealous of Kirsten. We talked it out, and once she got through the anger, she admitted that this was her biggest fear, loving him and losing him.

I think Jamie sees Kirsten as having what Jamie thinks she's lacking – beauty, body, etc. Myself, I think Jamie's stunning – sexy and beautiful, with a personality to match. If she could see herself through my eyes for one minute, it would probably change her whole life. I've never been able to understand her obsession with turning men's heads. I'm sure that's part of the reason she fools around. She needs men to find her attractive.

I think Jamie's parents made too big a deal out of her blind eye. They pampered her and treated her as if she was handicapped, not capable of her actual potential. She grew up feeling damaged instead of beautiful. To top it off, her father was cool and had difficulty communicating. She told me she felt only his discomfort around her, and his judgement. Another reason, perhaps, that she thrives on men's attention.

When Jamie wanted to take dance seriously in high school, her parents talked her out of it, saying that she had to be realistic – she'd never get anywhere with it because of her eye. I know they were just trying to protect her from future disappointment, but they have no idea how much that hurt her. Regretfully, she took their advice.

Todd's focus on sex (he has whined about not getting any every time she's called home) has given Jamie a focus for her fear of loss. She doesn't think she's good enough for him to wait for, so this thing with Kirsten seems huge. Besides, it's much safer for Jamie to leave him now than to stick it out and face her fears. Talking with her about this pushed a few buttons for me. Why do we spend our lives thinking we're not good enough, trying to change ourselves so people will love us and be attracted to us? Isn't the right person going to love us unconditionally, regardless of our looks and imperfections? It was all worth a good old chat anyway, and whether it was talking it out or the wine, Jamie was feeling better by the time we cycled back to the campsite. On the way, she hit the road barrier ha ha ha ha ha but managed to survive.

We sat outside the tent for a while, smoking in the pitch black. In fact, we couldn't see each other until one of us took a puff and the glowing ember lit up our faces. Jamie was battling with the hiccups when I first heard the rustling in the bushes. I freaked. Then I could hear it walking towards us, "skoosh skoosh skoosh" through the wet grass. "It's probably a RAT, god I HATE RATS - what is it Jamie?" I felt so vulnerable in the dark. "It's not a rat Larry," Jamie says, walking toward it with her flashlight while I stayed perched half in and half out of the tent, hand gripping the zipper. "It's a hedgehog. Come and look. He's REALLY cute!" A hedgehog? What's a hedgehog? (I'd heard of them but never seen one). Is it a member of the rat family? Jamie finally coaxed me over with all her oohing and awing, and she was right - It was SO CUTE!! It looked like a little Disney character - I swear it batted big long lashes at us. It looked us over for a few minutes and then turned and skooshed back the way it had come. Just a friendly neighbour come to check out all the racket I guess.

May 23

A quiet, relaxing day in Cambridge. Wrapped it up with dinner at Pizzaland and the movie "Pretty Woman" at a local cinema. Entertaining I guess, but in the end just another can't get it together myself, damsel-in-distress, saved by the rich handsome hero story. A great message to young women everywhere.

May 24

Weird dreams last night. More fear, but also family judgement, and victim stuff. Why do I see the family, in particular Mom, as being my judge? Why do I feel so certain that I'll never be totally happy or feel free to be myself as long as I live near her? So what if we don't have the same beliefs or values? So what if I'm not the daughter I think she may have wanted – one who likes to shop, wear dresses, and plan weddings? So what if we don't agree on everything? Aren't most families like that? Why do I feel guilty about it? And why do I try so hard to get her approval? I make myself sick sometimes, because I know that's what I'm doing. I know she loves me. She shows it to me in so many ways, and I know she's proud of me too.

During the Transformational Therapy course, I realized that I had an issue about hurting her, ever since Nathan died and I watched her scream over his tiny body. A regression showed me that I may have made a decision then not to let my loved ones suffer – but why do I think that I can hurt my mom just by being myself? What's wrong with me? Is it the drugs and alcohol? I'm not exactly a cokehead or an alcoholic, and she already knows about the pot.

So what is it? Why do I want to run away from my own family? How can I love and miss them so much, yet think I might be happier living in another country? It makes me feel terrible.

A late start but made great time on our 34-mile ride to Gosfield Lake. Stopped along the way for a gross chicken burger lunch that I burped up all afternoon. The campsite is nice, but we're right next to a graveyard, which is a bit spooky. I don't mind them in the daytime anymore. At first I wouldn't go in them at all. I'd sit out front while Jamie and Jo wandered around reading the headstones. I don't like walking on the graves.

I finally did go in one though, somewhere west of Oxford I think. It looked so ancient; I couldn't resist my curiosity. It was so sad. Whole families that had died within days of each other. Lists of young children and babies, gone one by one. Imagine the parents' grief. I guess it was during the plague. The graveyard was its history and told us of a town dark with death. I could see it in my mind and though I felt a deep sadness, I was amazed at what humans can live through. Many died, but some had to carry on.

We had dinner in the pub, played some crib, and then got the heebie-jeebies walking past the graveyard in the dark. Jamie kept freaking me out, poking at me and making weird sounds. I should have yelled, "Bear." Finally crawled into bed, tired, and realized we were on a slope again.

May 25

I had a bizarre dream about witches. They found out I knew about them and was writing about it in a book, so they were trying to get it from me. I was scared but knew I had to get the book to Ms. Wilson. I finally got it to her and she listened quietly, calmly thumbing through the book. She told me not to worry, that she'd take care of things. I was scared and thought about leaving town, but I trusted Ms. Wilson and thought we could take some kind of action together. I later became suspicious that she was one of them and found out she was. She told me it was okay, that they weren't evil, just mischievous sometimes. I walked around the town, in the grocery store etc., seeing how normal it was and knowing they were all witches. I was thinking it's okay, not bad – would I become one, and how? But then wondering if it was all a lie, that it was evil, and I'd find out too late. Started getting scared again, wanting to trust the woman, not wanting her to be bad or dangerous. Woke up afraid.

What am I afraid of? And why did I dream about Ms. Wilson? Why am I dreaming about our high school cooking teacher 11 years after graduation? Last night I was wondering what's wrong with me. They say everyone in your dream is a reflection of yourself. Do I think I might be evil? Ya right – a total nutbar seems more likely... Better leave the dream interpretation to the professionals.

And speaking of nutbars – I'll have to tell Jo I had a dream about our cooking class that didn't involve her slipping fried ants into my cake batter...

Man I'm tired of crappy sleeps - hips aching, legs & knees cramping, sliding down the hill into the wall of the tent, snorasaurus sawing logs in my ear. BUT - WE'RE GOING TO JANE'S FOR 3 OR 4 NIGHTS IN A BED!! WAHOO! Cold and windy today, so after running around in that dribbly shower trying to get wet, we hung out in the tent and updated our journals over tea and toast from the camp cafeteria. Only 21 miles to Chelmsford, so no rush.

We arrived in Chelmsford about 6:30 pm. Jane and Philip are great! She's Jamie's mom's best friend - and she's so funny! She talks about when she can get at Philip's money. It's obvious they love each other dearly. He's a big, tattooed, rugby player with a gruff voice and a huge soft spot for his granddaughter Sarah (7), who's here for the weekend.

We all had dinner in a fish n' chip shop. Jane claims to be a terrible cook. We talked about culture, travel, and UK politics. Jane and Philip lived in Africa for 3 years while Phil worked there. They also lived on an island in Southeast Asia. In the photo's we saw, it looked beautiful, untouched - and the islanders looked sweet and fun. I'd love to do something like that. Later in the evening, Philip took us to his pub, which Jane said was too rough for her. We met more of Jamie's relatives and had a good time. Phil left early, quite drunk, and we were feeling pretty good ourselves by the time we got back. Jane was watching a movie when we came in, so we sat up talking with her until quite late. She told us some great stories about herself and Jamie's mom when they were young. She also told Jamie about how strong her mom had to be, left on her own with the three kids when Jamie's dad went off to Canada to try and start a life for them there. Before I fell asleep, I thought about all the families including my own ancestors who crossed the Atlantic into the unknown - with great hope for a better life.

I have mixed feelings about that, because of the horrors of colonization. I admire the courage and strength it must have taken for people to move to Canada, where they'd have to build everything themselves, and where nothing was certain. They faced the dangers of the cold, the wilderness, and the hardships of the land. But it sickens me to think about what the settlers and their churches and government did to the First Nations people – pushed them off their land, denied them their livelihood, forced them to adapt to European culture, punished them for speaking their own language or practicing their traditional customs, kidnapping their children and abusing them in harsh residential schools. This is my heritage! When I first learned that, I felt ashamed and wished I was from a more humane race. I couldn't separate myself from the actions of my ancestors. Later, when I heard my gentle dad, who would never hurt anyone, say he sometimes felt ashamed to be a white man, I realized we don't have to feel guilty for what our ancestors did – we just have to be better than them. We have to make it right. We have to act responsibly, and not contribute to continued oppression. Speaking out against racism is essential, but we also have to acknowledge and eliminate institutional racism, which is harder to see from the privileged perspective.

Someone pointed out to me that every race has its horrors, its times of cruelty toward others, or negative aspects within its communities which involved the mistreatment of some members (women, other tribes, etc.). I suppose that could be true, but why is it that the caucasian race went all over the world treating anyone different as if they were less deserving of respect? Look at slavery, my god! What was wrong with those people's heads – or missing from their hearts? Was there a dominate and exploit gene?

May 27

Quote of the day: As we sat down to an elegantly decorated table, tantalizing aromas tugging at our appetites from the steaming plates of food, Jane told us that Philip had been cooking all afternoon to prepare his specialty just for us. "His specialty?" I asked, curious. "Baaa," Jamie whispered quietly in my ear – an impish, yet somewhat uncomfortable grin across her hung-over face. I kicked her under the table and tried not to laugh. Doomed to politeness, I picked up my knife and fork and looked down at my plate. "But they're my new friends…" I thought guiltily. Jamie grinned at me, so I booted her again and smiled back. Jeez.

Later on, Jamie and I had an interesting talk about eating meat, and vegetarianism. Jamie was surprised when I announced that I'm going to become a vegetarian when we get home, but she said she's thought about it too. I don't want to participate in the inhumane practices of the meat industry. Heather was telling me about the cruelty of factory farms – chickens raised with no room to move around or any chance to see the light of day; their beaks cut off so they won't peck each other to death in their over-crowded sheds; cows sick and suffering from unnatural diets of grain and corn – and being impregnated to keep them producing milk – only to take away their young within hours of birth and kill the males (often for veil) because they won't grow up to be milk machines. It's so sick – we are so sick. I don't understand how I can know this and then tune it out and eat meat as though I was a different person who'd never heard it. It's argued that humans are omnivores. I would argue that some are omnivores and some are herbivores. It will probably always be this way and I don't want to judge meat eaters any more than we judge animals that are carnivorous. But must the choice to eat meat be at the expense of our humanity – and our consciousness? How many meat eaters are consciously aware that they're eating animal flesh when they sit down to a steak dinner? How many give a thought to the life that was taken for it? I think there's a wall of denial around meat eating that makes it easy for factory farms to get away with such horrors. The meat and dairy industries take advantage of our denial and do whatever it takes to maximize profits. What kind of a world do we live in where making money is more important than our humanity?

May 30

It's been a great stay in Chelmsford. We met some wonderful people, saw the sights (a gypsy caravan on the side of the road where they're working in the fields; country roads and thatch cottages; parks and a reservoir that people swim and motorboat in??) Memorable moments: Talking with Tracy and Bill, two very gentle souls, taking a year off to sail to South America; Visiting Jane's parents and when she was trying to explain something to her 83-year-old dad and he finally got it her mom said, "Oh, the penny's dropped." They were so cute – and he'd been a cyclist all his life, only giving it up 3 years ago; Waking up all night itching after discovering small bugs everywhere in the loft; Jamie's announcement that we were having "snake and pigmy pie" for dinner (steak and kidney); Getting absolutely baked on a joint Jamie scored the night she stayed at the pub by herself – which somehow entitled her to woof almost our entire package of chocolate covered cookies while we prepared dinner for Jane and Philip.

Quote of the day: Jamie to Jane, "Oh we won't be drinking on the ferry. We have a big ride tomorrow, so we'll be going to bed early."

We left about 2:45 pm, excited to be on our way to the continent – Amsterdam here we come... Woo hoo! It was about 35 miles to the ferry and we made good time, less than 3 hours. I'm surprised how strong my legs are getting; I'm only 5 minutes behind Jamie these days. Nothing to do until the ferry at 9:00, so we went to a pub for munchies and drinks. We had a buzz on by the time we boarded the ferry – and full bladders. We locked up our bikes as fast as we could, hopping up and down and holding ourselves while we quickly grabbed just what we needed instead of taking the time to unhook our pannier bags. That was our first mistake.

From parking to reception, and up yet another floor, we winced and bounced around until we found a restaurant. We ran in, red-faced and arms full of stuff, and were met by a grinning waiter who didn't have to be asked. He just pointed us to our relief. Thank god. We settled into our berth (bunks and a bathroom), laughing about our grand entrance aboard this surprisingly fancy ship. "Attention Ladies and Gentlemen, the esteemed Larry and Larry have just arrived... in case you hadn't noticed."

We headed to the 2nd class bar where we drank, danced, and chatted. First to 4 Dutch guys, then to 4 young guys from New

York, then to two other Dutch guys, which is when I decided to do my Snagglepuss impersonation, "Exit, stage left - even", and go get some sleep. Jamie stayed.

May 31

I heard someone bang on the door, called Jamie, and obviously fell back to sleep. Woke up again and looked at my watch - 8:00 am. Went into the bathroom, poking my head back out to see if Jamie was there because it struck me that I couldn't remember letting her in. While I was brushing my teeth and trying to remember our arrival time, some guy came in and yelled at Jamie, "You have to get up, it's 8:00." She said, "ya, ya" and when I came out he was gone and she was asleep again. Then I remembered - we were scheduled to dock at 7:00 am! God, I was so hung over and in need of sleep I could hardly think, but when it hit home, I panicked.

I started shouting at Jamie and throwing my clothes on. "C'mon, we've been docked for an hour, we gotta get off or we'll end up back in England, hurry up!" She jumped up quickly, but was extremely slow getting her stuff together. I looked out the door and saw the place abandoned. The room doors were all open, carts of clean sheets in the hall. I looked out a porthole down the hall and it looked like we were moving. I stuck my head in the room door and yelled, "JAMIE, the boat's moving, we're leaving." I looked out again and saw that it was the boat beside us that was moving - oops!

I finally got Jamie out of there - she seemed like she was still drunk. We headed for the elevator and accidentally got in two different ones. I got to the bikes, but Jamie got lost for a while. I noticed right away that one of my panniers seemed empty on top and opened it to find that someone had stolen the big purple sweater Mom gave me. I loved that sweater - and now I don't have anything warm. Some people - man! Couldn't they see that I'm camping - that I'm only carrying the bare necessities? What an asshole! And what an idiot I am for leaving my stuff there in the first place. They could've taken everything. By the time Jamie showed up we were both fuming.

We were the last two off the boat, cycling past the cars loading for the trip back. We stopped at the terminal cafeteria for tea and toast. I spent 6 bucks on dry toast, an orange pop, and a cup of tea. They wouldn't give us anymore hot water and boy did they pick the wrong day to be messing with Jamie. She had a few "words" with the manager – and I'll tell ya, her breath alone probably made the guy wish he hadn't come to work this morning.

Once she cooled down, I told her that I couldn't remember letting her in last night. "YOU DIDN'T!" she fired back, as if I'd just smacked her. She told me that she came back to the room about an hour after me. She banged and banged on the door but I didn't answer. She ended up peeing her pants and left a little puddle on the carpet in front of the door. I still wouldn't answer so she had to go get someone to open the door with a master key. She was so embarrassed because she had to go all the way to the reception desk with wet pants – and bring them back to the puddle in front of the door! I burst out laughing when she told me, but quickly stuffed it when she aimed her Marvin Martian evil glare at me. Man – I'm surprised she didn't give me a good kick on her way up to the top bunk. But wait'll I tell Jo... HA HA HA HA – Too funny!

Jamie wanted to put up our tent at the edge of the ferry terminal and sleep, but I talked her into catching a train into Amsterdam. I just wanted to get there and cycling seemed out of the question.

Amsterdam is amazing. I was captivated the minute we got off the train. My first foreign language country! Central Station is a gorgeous old building, which sits at the north end of the city. Running south from it is the Dam Rak, a busy street crowded with restaurants, businesses, and signs, signs, and more signs! The feeling of being far from home was enhanced by the foreign print, European architecture, cable cars, and the murmur of an unknown language. It was mesmerizing.

The hostel is okay, but expensive – about $30 each. We showered and went off to eat and explore. Pizza on the Dam Rak cost almost $30 as well and they wanted $5 for a large coke. Ouch! We're going to have to be really careful with our money now. I spent a lot more than I'd wanted to our first month – too much drinking and eating in pubs. Now, it'll break us if we keep that up.

We got a message from Jo at our hostel, so we called her and made plans to meet. She's staying near the station and has already met some nice people. She traveled straight to Holland from Edinburgh. Once here, she took a side trip to Belgium, and told us that it was wonderful. She recommended Brugge, if we can get there. We were talking about the new challenges we'll be faced with now like not being able to read the menus and she told us that she paid $12 for mushrooms on toast in Belgium – and she thought she'd ordered fries and salad!

Jo took us to the street that people showed her for coffee shops (hash bars). We went in one and were all nervous about asking for it even though we could see and smell people smoking. Jo ordered "space cake" off the menu (as I winced at where that could lead), and asked the waitress about buying hash. She pointed out a guy so I asked him and he took me to a booth in the back. He went inside and handed me a menu through the little window. A drug menu! It listed different types of hash and pot and the price per gram. I picked Red Leb, one of the mid-priced ones. We smoked a joint and left for a drink at Jo's hostel pub because the coffee shops don't sell alcohol.

We ate and had a couple drinks with an Ethiopian woman and a couple of girls from Oregon. Jamie got pissed quickly (probably still on last night's dose). An American guy joined us later and we all went for a walk to a coffee shop called The Grasshopper. We ordered some "Super Skunk" at $25 for 1.8 grams and smoked a joint. Holy brain-frap, Batman…

We walked the streets with the rest of the tourists until we got to the red light district, a few blocks east of the Dam Rak. I couldn't believe what I saw. On the way, the streets started changing until they were all sex shops – paraphernalia, videos, live sex shows with men coaxing people in, some displaying a young woman out front. Then the streets with women in windows, sitting in lingerie or topless, the rooms lit by red light. The canals have red lights strung across them and the narrow streets were packed with tourists, looking at the women while they munched on pizza and slurped ice cream. I couldn't believe it! I didn't know how I felt. I was stunned at the amount of people. It's a major tourist attraction. In fact, the area seems like a big carnival – food stands everywhere, souvenirs (most referring to sex). Seeing the women made me feel embarrassed, angry, sad, and in the end – nothing. I went home (stopping to eat chips, chocolate, and fries with mayo – mmm!) feeling like it had been a strange dream.

June 1

Started the day off feeling tired and I have a sore throat. Went with Jamie and a girl from LA to a coffee shop. They offered us a drug menu – with little samples of pot and hash taped to it!! Not for breakfast thanks...

The three of us went to Anne Frank's House together. I started to feel more comfortable on the street. I realized last night that a lot of the people on the street are tourists and that this drug/sex thing isn't like it would be at home. It's more accepted by the people who live here and for everyone else it's just a curiosity.

There are lots of cool people here. I love the way they ride their bikes. There are thousands of bikes, and they have their own roads, paths, and traffic lights. We quickly learned that a ringing bell means, "Move fast or die", because they don't slow down. Most of them look the same – old black rickety one speeds – but there are some groovy painted ones too. Apparently bike theft is high. I guess it's easy when they can't be easily distinguished. Some of them are modified with extended fronts for carts. I've seen people carrying babies, groceries, guitars, and huge plants. Everyone seems to be moving so quickly, but they look so casual at the same time. Some have a buddy hanging off the back rack – or standing on it! They don't even hold on, just bounce along at a good speed. It's cool! The city seems as though it wasn't really built for cars. Except for the Dam Rak, the streets are very narrow.

So, we went to Anne Frank's house. It was sad. She was so young – and locked away for two years! It was uncomfortable to be in the room where they lived, thinking of them being there, of her writing in her journal, dreaming of being a writer someday. I felt sick when they told us she died in a concentration camp one month before liberation. Images of the camps flashed in my mind for a long time after we left, and when we were in the street again, it seemed different. These streets, these buildings – Nazis and terrified people! Some dragged from their hiding places, never to return. It's amazing that people can continue to believe in a god when things like this happen in the world.

In the afternoon, Jamie and I picked up some food and went to a park. We wanted to get away from the crowds and the junk food for a while, so we picked a park on the map that was away from the action. Unfortunately, it wasn't much of a park - more like (as Jamie put so eloquently) a "Poo Gallery". "And over 'ere we 'ave zee piece de resistance…" Ahem. Enough already. We got high, then each picked a bench and tried to write some postcards. That didn't work, so off we went in search of waffles with chocolate and about 4 inches of whip cream.

I realized yesterday how my road navigation for Jamie and myself has grown to the point that I am directing her in the city as well. Go this way, go that way, it cost this much, we have to do this, etc. I was leading her in every way. She doesn't try to remember how to get around or think about what she wants to do or how to do it. She relies on me. She doesn't know how to get back to the youth hostel. Last night, when we were walking home, she was ahead and she'd go to make a wrong turn and I'd say, "No, go left" or "Keep going". It made me feel so weird! Thinking about it today, I realized that I don't want to be responsible for another person on this trip. I want to be a good friend, but I don't want to be taking care of everything, making all the plans. God, I feel guilty just thinking of stepping out of that role.

So I talked to Jamie about it. She said she didn't think it was such a bad thing. I told her I didn't think it was bad, but I didn't feel comfortable about it. I tried to be diplomatic and not hurt her feelings. I said it made me feel bossy, and I didn't like that.

I tried to let Jamie lead for a while, and make decisions. It lasted about 20 minutes before I was doing it again because she was lost and we were going all over the place. This isn't going to be easy. I adore Jamie, but I don't want to spend my whole Europe trip like this.

I really don't know how to solve this. Maybe I should go to Berlin instead of south with them. I have mail to pick up and the break would give me the chance to step out of this. Jamie would learn that she doesn't need me and when we meet later we can travel together, but be independent too. She'd probably be pretty upset if I decided to do that.

Later, we met up with Jo and her friends Gina and Carmen. Gina is Jo's work buddy, and seems to have the same sense of humour – a scary thought…

We walked around, found them some space cake, and had tea at the "Free Adam" coffee shop – great reggae! I enjoyed Carmen and Gina's company. Nice, funny, and it soon became apparent that they're a couple. I was surprised how comfortable they were, telling us about their plans to get married. I felt happy for them, but I also felt a little awkward and self-conscious. I guess I haven't been around many gay people. Or any? Oh and here's a coincidence – last night I told Jo about my scary dream with Ms, Wilson being in cahoots with evil people and she said she heard that Ms. Wilson left her husband for a woman! Thinking about that on the same day as meeting Carmen & Gina, I realize that I don't have a clue what gay people look like. I thought lesbians looked kind of tomboyish. But these women are not like that at all. Seems I have to be hit over the head with a stereotype before I realize I'm carrying one. And it seems traveling can bust down more than racial stereotypes…

We all ended up in a pub having a drink in front of an open window in the red light district. As we watched the tourists looking at the women, I noticed that a lot of them looked like I felt last night – embarrassed, taking quick glances and looking away, laughing nervously. I felt more comfortable – not embarrassed anymore. What a difference.

June 2

Slept in until 9:30. Still feeling really tired, and my sore throat seems to be getting worse. Hurried to pack up and sign out so we could meet Jo by 11:30. We decided to cycle south from Amsterdam, toward Hilversum, eventually crossing the German border near Cologne. It was flat and easy. Once out of the city, I felt myself relax into the wide-open space and calming colours of nature once again.

When we stopped for lunch, I stayed with the bikes while Jo and Jamie went into a grocery store. I assumed they'd shop for the three of us like before. I was starving. A while later Jo came out and said she'd got her own but Jamie had bread and cheese she might split with me. I went in and said, "What'd you get?" She didn't answer just pointed at it. I said, "What's the scoop?" She said she just got it for herself. I was surprised and hurt, and as I did my own shopping – kinda mad. For 5-6 weeks we've bought food together for lunches and camping. If she wants to change it fine – asserting her independence I guess – but tell me, instead of leaving me starving in the parking lot guarding her bloody bike!

In the midst of this huffing around, the funniest thing happened. Jamie had a bottle of water when I saw her in the store so I asked where she found it. She pointed me in the direction but I couldn't find the one she had and settled on another. Thank god. Outside in the parking lot, the Larry's munching at a safe distance from one another, Jamie cracked open her bottle of water and tipped her head back for a good long swig. No sooner had she done that – and she was spewing it out in a giant spray. I was too grumpy to ask, but I heard her tell Jo that it was VINEGAR!!

At the campsite outside of Amersfoort, Jamie and I ended up stuck in the tent while it poured rain. I feel a real need to be on my own for a while. I think it would do us both some good. She must feel the same. We've been together almost constantly for six weeks now.

We smoked our last joint for a while (crossing the border tomorrow), wrote postcards, and then started laughing about Jamie eating everything in sight. That led to the funny of the day and we laughed ourselves silly over that one. I don't think I'll ever forget the sight of her spewing that vinegar. A classic Larry moment!

June 3

Puddles in the tent.

We decided to take the train to Cologne (Koln) from Amersfoort and get quickly through these expensive countries. We can go to Portugal early and spend more time there. Jo's bike fell over going down the stairs and nearly crushed her. Then it was so high to lift it onto the train that she lost her grip and all her stuff fell down through the space between the train and the platform onto the tracks. Some guy got most of it with the hook of his umbrella, but she lost her lock. As I was noticing the people on the platform laughing, Jamie stepped in Jo's helmet and fell forward. Sometimes I feel like I'm traveling with Lucy and Ethel.

When we arrived at the hostel "Koln-Deutz", they put us in a 3-bedroom, which is nice but on the male dorm floor currently occupied by a group of young teenage boys. They're pretty loud and rambunctious. Could be a long night.

June 4

It was. They kept us awake half the night, yelling and slamming doors. Up at 7 am. Down to breakfast and found out they had a 3-bedroom on the girls' floor - a slight improvement in the day.

We went to the train station to change some money and get some info about going to Munich. It's cheaper to take the train than to do the Rhine cruise. Oh well, miserable weather anyway. We also found out that we can't take our bikes on all trains. We can ship them and wait 4-5 days. Forget that. Or, we can take them with us on the slow train that leaves at midnight and arrives at 7:00 am. If we waited until tomorrow that would mean walking around Koln with our bikes and gear from checkout at 9 am until 11pm. Forget it. I'm not doing another Swansea and the weather's bad. So I decided to leave tonight, even though I paid at the hostel. At least I have somewhere to relax and keep my stuff until the train leaves.

Jo decided to do the same and Jamie announced at lunch that she was definitely staying another night and was going to France or Switzerland. Getting concerned about money I guess. I was shocked and have mixed feelings. It will be the break we need. On the other hand, I'm a little nervous about cycling on my own. Jo will be going her own way in Austria to visit relatives and we decided we'd all meet in Lisbon on July 7th. From Austria, I'll be cycling through Switzerland, France, and Spain by myself!! I'm excited about it, but nervous... definitely nervous. All those mountains to get through, and on the road alone all day. What if something happens to my bike? I can't speak the languages... Geez, it'll be fine. I've got to break out of this. Meet more people. It's a perfect chance. It'll be good for me. So we bought our separate tickets.

Later, Jo and I went in the Cathedral "Kolner Dom". It was fabulous. It has survived 14 bombings, after being built in the 12th or 13th century. Incredible stained glass windows, paintings, carved statues, tapestries, and vaulted ceilings. Topped it off with our first German chocolate and went back to the hostel to rest and update our journals. The weather is just too gross for sightseeing, especially as none of us seem to be feeling that great.

Over dinner, I realized that it was bothering me that Jamie had changed plans without talking about it – and I feel disappointed that we won't see Austria and Switzerland together. I don't know why she won't talk about things. Maybe she's afraid of being on her own too.

Back at the hostel, Jo and I started packing up. Jamie handed over the cooking pot and said she wouldn't need it so she didn't want to pack it anymore. I was instantly upset. I said fine, leave it. I turned and left, but Jo followed me. She encouraged me to talk to Jamie about it before we left. I didn't think talking would do any good, and I wasn't even sure why I was so upset. It's my pot, which I bought (as well as the stove) for all of us to use. I'm carrying the stove, fuel, rice, peas, etc. Jamie just has to carry the pot. Assuming we'll need cooking stuff when we meet up again, shouldn't she have some of the load? It's just a stupid pot – but somehow it's more than that...

When I was packed, I asked Jamie to go for a smoke and talk. I couldn't say anything for a while so we sat there in silence. I finally told her I didn't want to leave on a sour note and that I was sorry I got upset about the pot. She said she didn't see why she should carry it when she wasn't using it. I said that we'd need it if we wanted to cook when we met up again. She said, "Will we meet up again?" I was stunned. Why wouldn't we? She said it didn't seem like we were too anxious to make meeting plans. But I'd spent most of my time in the restaurant figuring it out. Was I supposed to write it out for her too? She'd made the decision to split and she was going to be ahead of us. She could say where and when she'd be in Switzerland. It was her responsibility too. She said it was all BS; she didn't need it and wasn't going to take it. She was cold and shut off. When I looked at her, I felt like I didn't know who she was – at least this side of her. I was controlling my feelings, stopping myself from crying. I don't want to do almost everything anymore so she quits doing her little bit. I got up to leave and she said, "See you in the movies Bud." I got my bike and went outside.

When Jo came outside I said, "If you want to meet Jamie you better give her the addresses. She doesn't have them and we just said adios." She ran in and gave them to her. I rode to the station stuffing down my tears. When we got to the station, I told Jo what happened. She was really supportive and encouraged me not to judge my feelings. She tried to shed light on Jamie's actions by pointing out her difficulty communicating, and possible fear of being on her own.

I understood that and I could see that I'd got the ball rolling when I talked to her in Amsterdam about her dependence on me. I guess it's hard for us to let go of the safety of those roles. Maybe we're both scared. I thought of the kids at the group home and how they'd try to piss you off by doing something really rotten just before they got moved out. For some people, it seems to be easier to push someone away when you have to say good-bye.

Jo and I had beds on the train. I howled in giddy laughter as we desperately tried to get the doors to the luggage cars open and couldn't. Finally, a guy came along and helped. Then Jo got stuck between two guys in the narrow corridor, pulling them along with her overstuffed backpack. She also knocked a conductor and his bag of chips flying backward into his room after he pointed us in the right direction. I could barely see through the tears in my eyes from laughing so hard.

There were two girls from New Zealand in our sleeping car. They woke up and chatted to us for a bit. They told us not to let the conductor take our passports – "Whatever you do!" – but he wouldn't take no for an answer so we had to cough them up and then worry about it. When he handed them to us in the morning, we felt silly and wondered what the girls had been talking about. Oh well – we worried – and they suffered our "getting the flu gas". Poor things.

By the time we got off the train in Munich at 7:22 am, we had blazing fevers. We cycled painfully to the other side of the city only to find out that we were too old for the youth hostel. Damn. So back to tourist info at the station and booked a room in a pension for $30 /night. We were so happy when we finally got there at 2:30. Slept for a few hours, feeling very fluish – fever, chills, aching. When we woke up, we went out briefly to get some juice and food. Couldn't find much, but got a big bottle of apple juice and a take out dinner which we just picked at. The AJ was great though. We played crib and laughed about paying $30 /night to be sick. Oh well. To sleep early. Woke up a few times in the night, bad fever, sweating a lot – more than I ever remember.

June 6

Woke up soaked, but a little better. Aching gone. Now a wicked cold and still slightly hot. I almost called Jamie in Basel last night, my only chance before Portugal. I wanted her to know I still want to meet her. I wish I didn't feel so guilty, like I really let her down... If she's in Portugal, she is. If not, then it's not meant to be. This was all supposed to happen, I know that. We're each responsible for our own experiences. It'll work out. But I hope she'll be there...

We decided to go see the Neuschwanstein castle, and pretend we felt okay. We hopped a train to Fusson, a cute little village in the Bavarian Alps. The trip there was pretty – we saw our first cows wearing bells!! We bused up to the castle parking lot and hiked the 25 minutes up to the castle itself. The hike was tough with our congested chests and sinuses, but well worth the effort. It's amazing! A fairy-tale castle nestled in the mountains.

A very charming German guide escorted us through the inside. He was well informed and told us some of the stories of the castle. The royal who commissioned the construction of the castle is sometimes referred to as "Mad King Ludwig" because he was declared insane (his extravagance had supposedly pissed off some other royals). Ludwig and the psychiatrist that had certified him were later found drowned in shallow water. The mystery was never solved. "Because Sherlock was British," whispered Jo. "Sherlock was fictional," I whispered back. "I knew that," Jo whispered defensively, a puzzled look crinkling her forehead. "I did," she whispered again a few seconds later, purposely pushing me into the tour guide.

The castle is beautiful inside – lots of oak and marble, and the most incredible views from every window. I loved the catacomb hallway, and the solarium garden in particular. Jo, on the other hand, preferred the guide and his cute little... personality.

On the train ride back, we met two students from the States, studying in England and doing a whirlwind tour of Europe for their two-week break. They'd been to an amazing number of places, including Corfu, Greece where they'd had a bad experience. They were taken to a hotel way out in the boonies and the guy wouldn't bring them back. They were sweet. When we said good-bye, they said they'd say a prayer for us. Though I thought it sounded like they needed it more than we did, I was touched. Their good-heartedness I guess.

June 7

We caught the 9:20 train to Salzburg, birthplace of Mozart and backdrop for The Sound of Music. The scenery was pretty in the mountains and the ride was less than two hours. On the way to the hostel, we met a representative for "Let's Go Europe". He asked us for tips on cycling in Austria, but since we'd just arrived we told him we'd write if we had any good info. At the hostel, we booked into an 8-bed room and shared travel stories with some of our bunkmates. Everyone has an interesting tale or two. It's fun to sit around and listen to them.

In the early afternoon, Jo decided to go to a doctor for some antibiotics so I waited down in the hostel lobby for her. I met Chang, a really nice Korean guy, who told me that in Korea bold girls like me (wearing shorts) would get many stares and whistles. He also said he lived near an American Army base and found it hard to watch the soldiers treating the Korean women disrespectfully. I was sorry to learn that the poor guy was robbed of a bag that contained about 20 rolls of undeveloped pictures, the only thing he had to show his family of his tour of Europe. I also met a girl from the US, taking a break from working in Italy for a two-month tour of Europe. It's great to meet all these people doing cool things like working or studying abroad – or spending their life savings to fulfill a dream.

A woman from Quebec City joined us at one point. I liked her right away and enjoyed talking to her. It was a little weird when she first approached us though. I saw her come in and found myself following her with my eyes as I talked to Chang. I wasn't thinking anything just noticing. I didn't see her face until she sat down across from me, and then she lifted her head and looked me straight in the eyes. My breath caught a bit when our eyes met, but the moment passed quickly as the conversation continued and she joined in. I didn't think about it again until now. That was really strange. Anyway, I felt really excited to be meeting and talking with people more than before.

When Jo got back, we went out in search of groceries and then had a picnic out front. She took a nap after that and I sat in the lounge and worked on my journal. The French woman, Anik, joined me and we talked about our mutual schooling and interest in psychology. She has a great attitude toward life. Her English is pretty good and it was fun to work around the words she didn't know. Her accent is really cute, but I didn't mention it. "Me, I 'ave no accent but my brudder, 'ee does dough."

Up to the room and relaxed with Jo for a while. We came downstairs at some point, trying to figure out what a long box was in the candy machine. Jo asked some girls about it and then said, "Riley thought it was men's underwear." Where does she come up with this stuff?

June 8

Wow – did I have a bizarre dream! I woke myself up throwing my knee up in the air (and blankets too). I was kneeing a guy who was trying to rape me. I had no energy to fight back, could hardly move, and it took everything I had to knee him. I don't remember much else, just fear and feeling helpless.

We did the "Sound of Music" tour today. It was fun – eight of us in a van, including our guide Peter who was very funny. He took us to the different sites of where the movie was filmed, and though it was pouring rain, we all had a good time. I had to refrain from hysterical laughter when he plugged in the movie soundtrack and some people started singing along to The Hills are Alive.

After dinner, I saw Jo sitting with Anik so I joined them and ended up taking Anik up on an invitation to join her for a classical music concert. I really like her. And it kind of feels as if we've been friends for years. Martine, a young woman from Montreal, joined us. The concert was sold out so we listened at the door for a while (though not before looking for a way to sneak in). Afterward, we walked around talking and went into a pub for a drink. Martine turned out to be only 18 – wow! Very knowledgeable and mature – and traveling Europe by herself! I was so surprised.

On the way back to the hostel, we talked about conditioning, youth, and how the world seems to be changing a bit for the better. Martine went to bed and Anik and I walked around a bit more. It was nice. We made plans to go hiking tomorrow.

June 9

Showered, dressed, and down in the breakfast room early. I was excited to meet Anik for breakfast and go on our hike. Jo was going on a walking tour with an American woman so Anik and I headed off without her, feeling good about the adventure ahead. We reached the base of the mountain at 10 am but couldn't find a trail, so we followed a guy with a dog and Austrian hiking poles. He led us to the trail, but I think he got a little suspicious because he kept looking over his shoulder at us.

We hiked up, stopping briefly to laugh about the trail disappearing (about 10 times). When it did, we went straight up through the bush until we came upon the trail again. I feel very happy and oddly connected with Anik. We're so comfortable together. We make each other laugh and have so much in common. I wanted to talk about so many things, and we did. I wish I could speak French. Sometimes we have difficulty due to the language barrier; mostly it's hard for her to find the English words to express her feelings. I can see it's frustrating and tiring to not be able to speak in French. I suggested she tell me in French because although I wouldn't understand the words, I'd hear the feeling. God, the stupidest things just fall right out of my mouth sometimes – she probably thinks I'm an idiot.

We reached the top at 1:00 pm, long after the seniors club had sprinted past us while we were catching our breath on a steep incline. Jeez, have they got fuel injection in those poles, or what? The view was beautiful from the 1286 m peak, with Salzburg tucked into the valley below. We watched some hang-gliders take off, and had a picnic. Anik's foot was bothering her and it became cold so we tried to hitchhike back. When that didn't work out, we decided to walk down, but stick to the trail this time. On the way down, two deer appeared on the trail in front of us. I love that wonderful quiet… just the sound of your heart, your breath, and the animal's soft departure. It started to rain and the trail was getting muddier by the minute. We laughed about the likelihood of one of us falling as it was quite steep and slippery. I said, "If someone falls it will probably be me." She said "Probably." I like her more by the minute. She's intelligent and passionate about life and politics in Quebec. It's interesting to meet someone with such convictions. She's so independent and strong in her beliefs, very outgoing and comfortable being herself. She looks me right in the eye when she talks to me and I like it. We're friends already. It's like a magnet. I've never experienced anything like it. Kind of strange really.

On the way down the trail, we somehow ended up at a field. We walked through it, grass to our chests, feet sinking and soaking in water. Laughing. It was pouring. We went through a dense grove of trees and down a muddy slope and guess what? Anik got to the bottom and looked up at me. She said wait and moved to the side holding up her arms in a blocking gesture, laughing. I said, "ya right," and then slid down and landed flat on my back in the mud. I lay there and laughed. She said she knew it would happen, that she could see the future. I was absolutely covered in mud. We were both drenched and our feet made squishing sounds in our shoes.

We finally spotted a road, but had to cross another field to get to it. I checked my compass (oops, forgot I had it), and we were on the opposite side of the mountain that we wanted to be on. How had that happened? So we sludged down the highway laughing about this crazy country and rotating mountains. I must have been quite the site covered in mud. Cars honked and Anik insisted on walking behind me for the humorous view. The road eventually brought us in sight of the city, but started going around it so we climbed over a fence and went down a steep hill into yet another deep, wet field. We couldn't stop laughing as we dragged ourselves through the city. We imagined all the locals shaking their heads at the loser tourists. "Another couple of fools lost the trail" (presuming of course that this could happen to someone else).

Not far from the hostel, an Italian guy came up and asked me for a date. He either had a good sense of humour or very bizarre taste. Into mud-wrestlers pal? He was funny. He said, "Do you have a boy?" I said no so he said, "Well?" and held his arms out, looking down at his body. I laughed and shook my head, running to catch up with Anik. She commented that she doesn't like guys that just want sex. I agreed, though I didn't see the relevance. This was just funny, maybe because a woman in Dublin told me Italian guys can be like that. I wonder what it's like to travel in Italy?

When we got back to the hostel, I had to go straight to the front desk to pay for another night. In the meantime, Anik found Jo in the cafeteria and brought her out to laugh at me. Thanks new friend who seems like my old friends…

After changing, I called home to wish Alex a happy birthday and talked to the whole family including Donna and Jessica. It was hard to hear Jessie because it was so noisy in the lobby. When I hung up, Anik was sitting in the lobby waiting. She wanted a drink and I hadn't eaten so we got ready to go out. I told her to keep the leather belt that I'd lent her to hold up her pants for the hike and she gave me a little daypack for future hikes.

We couldn't find a place to eat so we ended up in a cozy little pub where I got drunk rather quickly on my empty stomach. We talked about boyfriends, relationships, family, etc. It was nice and I felt sad that we'd be going in separate directions the next day. We swapped addresses and she encouraged me to come to Quebec on my way home from Europe – to see the autumn colours.

On the way back to the hostel Anik asked me if I'm happy with my life. I told her that what keeps me from being totally happy is my inability to be myself around my family and friends. What?? Anik didn't seem to notice that I was a bit stunned by my own answer. She was sweet and encouraged me to be myself – to find out they'll love me for who I am. Drawing a blank now – like a heavy fog rolled in.

June 10

I heard people so I got up to shower and not miss breakfast. Hung over. After my shower, I looked at my watch and it was only 6:30 am. Jeepers! Packed up and went downstairs. Anik came in shortly after 7 and we laughed about our sore heads. She walked to the station with Jo and I. There wasn't a train to Zurich or Lucerne that would take my bike so I made a quick decision to go to Vienna with Anik. We took the same train as Jo and Margaret, the American that Jo had been spending time with. The four of us had fun chatting and the time passed quickly. Jo and Margaret had a reservation in Vienna and Jo is cycling to her relative's tomorrow morning, so we went our separate ways at the station.

Anik and I spent some time on the phone, unable to find a place that wasn't booked for a week. I put my bike in storage and we walked toward city centre. All we could find was a pension for $30 each. Too expensive but no choice. It's a nice room with a tub and shower. We had a spaghetti dinner in a little restaurant. Anik was upset by an article in a French newspaper that said that Quebec officials had reached some kind of agreement with the Canadian government so separation wouldn't happen. Good dinner though. I'm curious about her political opinions and respect her commitment, but politics don't interest me in the least. None of the parties represent what I value and I don't want to spend my life upset about that. A cop-out maybe, but I do vote. After dinner, we picked up a bottle of wine and headed back to the room as it was pouring again.

Somehow we went too far and missed our room. Passed it again on the way back. Hilarious. First they rotate mountains and now they're moving our hotel room. Finally found it and relaxed with wine and chatted.

Later, I enjoyed a nice hot Fa bath and after Anik had had hers, we chatted from our beds. She asked me to read her an article out of the French newspaper. She said my pronunciation was pretty good, but I think it was more entertaining by the smile on her face. During the evening, I was feeling more and more drawn to being closer – to being near her. It was overwhelming, and it made me feel pretty weird.

June 11

It was another great day with Anik. I feel like I've known her always. We laugh a lot and tease each other. I love it when she says, "Where we are?" with her cute French accent.

Vienna is beautiful. I'm so glad I decided to come. The history experienced through the architecture and the art is quite amazing. I've never seen such huge sculptures – chariots, horses, and angels the size of small buildings! Our sightseeing cram included the Sigmund Freud Museum (boring), and St. Stephen's church, which was a surreal experience. The outside, like a lot of these old churches, is dark and harsh looking. Trying to take a picture, I had to back up a block (a little more, a little more, oh just a little more, hey I'm back in Salzburg), just to get in one of the spires – "just" the spire that is, not the church. I would've had to go to Germany to get the whole thing in.

The inside took my breath away, but as I walked around, taking more in, my mood changed. I was touched by the sight of this magnificent love of God, but also sad. If people loved their neighbours and the earth as much, what a different world it would be.

I was standing in front of a cherub pierced with thorns when Anik walked up. And then I suddenly saw the flames. I felt the fear and the rage rising up. The emotion thudded in my chest and filled my eyes. I turned away from Anik, not wanting her to see how I was feeling. Knowing I couldn't explain. Outside, I lingered near the church for a bit. I felt crazy. That scene, those feelings... Since finishing Nadja's course, they've become a distant memory, like an old dream I barely remember. Bizarre that it would come up now, after all this time – and so dramatically. And why? I never thought about the fact that I'd be here in Europe where Joan had lived, and died... And I don't really want to think about it now.

We caught a train to Lucerne after I made arrangements for my bike to be shipped there. I hate it not being on the same train as me. We've never been separated before... I feel so, so... pathetic?

I had a totally embarrassing moment today. We were walking down the street talking and I looked at Anik and one of those emotion bubbles came out of my chest into my eyes (like during a touching scene in a movie). She saw it right away and said, "You're laughing in your eyes." I said, "My heart is smiling." Good god, what am I doing? I'm possessed by a sappy weirdo. I think I should go my own way soon.

June 12

Off the train in Zurich at 8:25 am for a transfer to Lucerne at 9:00. My pannier bags are a hassle, and I spilled coffee in my helmet. My cycling stuff definitely isn't convenient for train travel with Anik. So I decided to buy a backpack. Arrived in Lucerne at 9:50, threw my stuff in a locker and went to tourist info and the bank. It's rainy so we can't see the Alps! I can feel them though, lurking behind the clouds, towering and tremendous. The cool, crisp air gives them away. What a disappointment to not find them waiting for me. Should have called ahead I guess...

We walked around the town chomping on a family-size package of Swiss chocolate bars. The streets are narrow, no cars, and the buildings are nicely decorated with paintings and pretty flower boxes under the windows. Just how I thought Switzerland would look. I only wish it wasn't raining.

When we were walking around Anik asked, "Did I, like a pig last night? Don't know the word in English." I just looked at her, not having a clue what she was talking about – until she demonstrated a snore. "Not that I noticed," I answered sincerely (ya right, who wouldn't notice? But it was more like a bear). She also told me today that her father drowned when she was seven, stuck under a capsized boat. And then at nine, she saw her friend drown. I didn't know what to say.

When we checked into the hostel, Anik got the last bed and I got a mattress on the floor. We showered and relaxed with tea while we wrote in our journals. It feels so good to be with her.

June 13

I woke up in the middle of the night, rolled over, and looked toward Anik's bed. Just then, she sat up and looked at me, smiled, and lay down again. I rolled over and went back to sleep, happy. It seemed natural in that moment, today it seems totally bizarre. We have some kind of connection. I can't explain it.

My bike hasn't shown up yet, so I made arrangements for them to forward it to Madrid. That will give me time to recoup a little more from my cold – and travel with Anik a little longer. We decided to head for sunshine on the French Riviera. It doesn't look like the rain's going to let up soon, so we're off to Nice. We did some laundry (Fifteen bucks!) and caught the afternoon train to Geneva. The ride was great. At least we got to see some mountains, and the green valleys of Switzerland are gorgeous even in the rain. We talked about music and books and she let me listen to her French music (Harmonium), which went great with the view.

In Geneva, we walked around for about five hours, seeing as much as we could, talking, laughing, and in some moments, probably not caring where we were at all. We had dinner at Pizza Hut. Shameful I know, but it's unbelievably expensive here. I paid $4 for a coke! Anik forgot the map in the restaurant, so we got lost again.

We bumped into Martine, also on her way to Nice, so we teamed up in a cabin on the train. The seats pulled out just a little making two beds – so Anik and I shared one side and Martine ended up sharing her side with some guy who came in the middle of the night. Just before Anik fell asleep she started complaining about her elbow being sore. She had what didn't look like more than a scratch, but it was obviously infected. She broke out in a fever and was blazing most of the night. Some backpackers were partying in the next cabin so I got little sleep. (Funny how they're "idiots" when you're not in the party mood). I checked Anik's forehead a lot and kept her covered up. It was kind of nice.

June 14

Woke up to a French woman throwing open the door and curtains, and saying something about crochettes? She sat down, throwing our stuff out of her way and started reading a paper. Talk about a rude awakening ... we sat there quite dumbfounded for the first few minutes, squinting into the brightness, hair askew, not sure whether she was done yet. I'm sure we were all thinking the same thing ("What a bitch!"), but not one of us so much as peeped. Her aggressive confidence was intimidating. So we glared behind her paper and silently dared her to say another word.

The good side was that now we weren't missing the gorgeous ride into Nice – the beautiful red stone coastline, and blue, blue water. Upon arrival, we hit the beach for some topless sunburning and a much needed nap. Anik had refused our advice to go to a doctor, but by afternoon her elbow was red and swollen half way up her arm. We went to a pharmacist who took one look and scribbled down a doctor's address. His concern was the last push she needed. I went into the doctor's office with her and although I couldn't understand a word, I could tell it was serious. Turned out to be blood poisoning and it was almost up to her armpit. Scary. She got a prescription for some strong antibiotics.

Spent the afternoon sightseeing – mostly shops and tourists but a few nice spots. Had a good dinner at a Chinese cafe and went to bed early. Another great day!

June 15

Hard not to wake up happy when greeted by Anik's smiling face and loving eyes. But I'm getting too attached and that's not a good thing – too complicated and too weird. I have to pull myself out of this somehow.

We had breakfast with Martine at the casino cafeteria and then went our separate ways; Anik and I caught a train to Cannes. We walked through the old city and it was so cool. Narrow, alley-like streets, high buildings, pastel shutters, laundry hanging colourfully, quiet... I loved it. I could live there. Later, we met Martine again and took a bus to Miramar, which was interesting. The driver was really nice, and cute, but he drove like a bat out of hell on those narrow winding roads. Another 10 minutes and I would've been hanging out the window. Fortunately, I made it and still enjoyed the view along the coast. The red rock against the turquoise water is awesome. This is the best! Paradise.

We found a private little cove to eat our lunch and go for a swim. Anik found a cave and swam into it. She'd no sooner disappeared when I heard her yell and she came flying out in a splash of arms and legs, cutting her foot on a rock in her panic. "A tarantula" she explained. "Uh-huh," I teased, as she clambered onto the rocks. "It was DIS BIG', she demonstrated a little defensively, "and I urt my foot." Cute little Frenchie!

I swam out to a rock in my underpants and lay there, enjoying the feeling of the sun on my skin. It's so stupid that men can walk around topless all summer and women can get arrested if they do the same. It's ridiculous. It feels so good. Men are lucky.

I could've stayed there all day (and probably should have) but we had to catch the bus back to Cannes. On the bus, I asked Anik about her travel plans. Afterward, I felt angry at myself. I feel like I've lost control of myself – my feelings for this woman are affecting my trip. I realized I might do anything to stay with her – spend more money, change my plans, etc. I had pictures of us finding a way to stay somewhere, live or travel in one of these beautiful places we've seen. Stupid. And it makes me feel creepy. Sometimes when I'm with her, I find myself wanting to hold her hand or put my arm around her. When I sleep next to her, I find myself wanting to be closer. She's a woman. She's my friend. It makes me feel ashamed of myself.

So what do I do? I don't really want to run away, but I don't want to risk this unique friendship. There has truly never been anything like this before in my life. Such a magnetic and powerful connection. I know I shouldn't be angry with myself. I should feel how I feel and not judge it BUT I CAN'T HELP IT. Of course Anik picked up on it. She's always there. We constantly meet eyes and she reads every shift in my mood. No one has ever paid so much attention to me before, read me like that. I couldn't tell her, but she suggested we "take a coffee" later and talk. Maybe.

We got off the train in Nice to transfer to Monaco. Martine decided to pass. Monte Carlo was interesting to see. The palace and wonderful streets of Monaco with a view of Monte Carlo from the hill – a high-rise city all crowded into a small area set in the mountains. While we were checking it out from the hill, a storm rolled in. The clouds were incredible and it grew darker, windier. Lightning lit the sky in pink. Once again, the outside looked like the inside. Beautiful feelings swirling in fear, anger... electric, dangerous.

We walked to the station and watched the storm arrive. Jagged white lightning across a black sky, rain on the roof of the train. Can such powerful energy be contained? Obviously not. Within the hour, Anik and I were bent over bowls of rice when she asked me again what she'd seen in my eyes this afternoon. I struggled for quite a while, but finally explained how attached I'm feeling, my impulses to be affectionate, and how weird that makes me feel. She said she was upset because she could feel me pulling away, going inside. I cried. It hurt to acknowledge my feelings aloud, but later I felt kind of relieved. Anik was so sweet and she didn't judge me (or climb out the bathroom window). I really like her and I want to be free to enjoy this connection and not want any more than there is.

We talked for quite a while and then went back to the room. She asked me for a massage, which I was happy to give, but I didn't understand her asking me that right after I said how I felt. Maybe she doesn't really understand or, more likely, is not going to let it be a problem. Or perhaps... she's just a brat.

June 16

I woke up early and looked over at Anik. She said it was early, only 7:30, so to close my eyes for a while. I could feel her curled up behind me and it was hard to pull myself away, but I got up to shower.

In the shower I came to life. I remembered last night and felt strong. It's okay. I've just been confused by the intensity of our connection. I felt happy and sang, "I Feel Good". I met Anik back in the room with a smile. We packed up and went to the train station. We caught a train to Marseilles and transferred from there to Avignon. The French accents in Marseilles are quite different from other parts of France. I didn't need Anik to tell me that. I saw her stunned expression when she asked a train guy for directions. It was hilarious. Her face was so funny when she turned around and then she cracked up laughing. She hadn't understood a word he'd said.

Anik asked me on the train how I was feeling and I told her I feel good, everything is okay. She told me that she needs to think because she's lost track of what she's doing – she's thinking of going to Spain and Portugal and she knows it's because she wants to be with me. When she expressed these feelings to me, I looked in her eyes and my heart swelled with happiness and relief. YAY and PHEW !!!!! It's not just me! I felt two tears roll down my cheek. One for each of us, I thought. And then I laughed out loud at the total sap I have become.

I suggested that in Avignon, we take some time apart to think. I'm pretty sure I'll stay with her as long as I can, though I didn't tell her that. I want her to think about what she wants, and not to compromise her trip. I want her to be happy and not have any regrets.

Avignon is wonderful. It has an incredible, peaceful energy. I feel really comfortable here, calm and content. It's a spiritual calm, like nature evokes. It reinforces that everything is perfect as it is.

We had some trouble finding a room. The youth hostel is full and the rooms are expensive. We almost stayed with a couple we met on the street. We could get a good deal by sharing a room with two double beds. When we agreed, the couple went off to exchange some money. We paid and went up to the room. I stopped in my tracks outside the room when Anik pointed out a HUGE dead cockroach in the doorway. Anik walked around the inside trying to coax me in. "Cockroaches won't bother you," she said with confidence, "They're afraid of people. They only come out when the lights are off, and they'll never come on the bed" she assured me. "Can we sleep with the lights on?" I asked, looking around suspiciously. "Come on" she said, "You'll be fine." Feeling a little foolish standing in the hallway with my pack on while she got comfortable, I slowly took a brave step through the doorway. Just then, there was a huge scurrying noise. I jumped right back out into the hall. "That sounds like a pretty big cockroach to me," I winced. Anik poked her head around the corner into the bathroom. "That's not a cockroach," she said, "That's a rat." When she turned back to the doorway, I was gone. When she came (laughing) down the stairs to the lobby, she saw me standing on the other side of the street. She had tears rolling down her face when she approached me after stopping to get our money back. "It's not funny," I said defensively. "I hate rats."

We decided to sleep at the train station and tossed our stuff in a locker so we could get on with our sightseeing. Later, we ended up coming across a decent room for $40, so we booked it. We walked all over, enjoying the architecture and feel of Avignon. At the centre is "The Palace of Popes", a hangout for locals and tourists. The square was active with kids on skateboards, one laying on the sidewalk writing on the pavement with a felt pen. Four musicians filled the air with singing, drumming, and the delicate sound of a pan pipe. Yet for all these different sounds, there is still a silence here. The calming energy I sensed when we first arrived. Here it is the strongest. It makes me feel safe.

As we explored Avignon, I started to think about Joan of Arc and I realized I can't remember anything about her. Where was she born and when? When did she die, and where? I just draw a complete blank. It's really weird - I can't remember a bloody thing. Trying makes me feel frustrated and extremely tired.

June 17

I woke up early and puttered around until Anik woke up. I was feeling light-headed – I guess from not eating much yesterday. We dropped our packs off at the station and went in search of affordable food. Two and half hours later we found a cheap pasta place just in the nick before caving in and going to McDon'ts. I felt faint and would've paid anything for a meal but Anik refuses to spend more than she wants to. I want to save money too, but it seems worth the money to eat before the hungry headache and grumpys kick in. Anyway, we had a great meal and I stretched my shrinking stomach beyond its limits. I felt really tired afterward so I relaxed in the shade by the palace while Anik carried on. It was a scorcher of a day.

Anik came back shortly and we went for coffee to wake up. She told me she's decided to go to Barcelona with me but after that she will carry on alone. I said great, but I fought back the tears. She kept looking at me and asked if I was okay. I couldn't handle it so I told her I'd meet her in an hour and went for a walk. I tried to find somewhere I could be alone.

I've experienced feelings this week that I've never experienced before. For some reason we've been drawn together and we love each other although we only met 10 days ago. It feels so amazing to connect with someone in this way. I know it's natural to feel sad. But this is beyond the natural sadness of saying goodbye to a friend. I feel ripped apart. I feel weak, dependent, and ashamed.

As I walked, I could feel the black mire reaching out, clawing at me. It was stronger than usual. I wanted to strip off my skin, escape my body, run and run and run, leave the darkness far behind. I wanted to find a bar and drink myself unconscious. I wanted to take a magic pill that would turn the dark into light. I ran the rest of the way to the park.

I sat on the grass and soon felt the calm of Avignon wash over me. I breathed in the warmth of the sun and felt myself coming back a bit. As I looked out over the square, a young guy from Morocco joined me and was very sweet. He spoke Spanish and a little French. I understood some of the French. He asked if I wanted to smoke some hash, but I declined and started back toward Anik. God, I could've used that hash but I knew it wouldn't solve anything. I did feel better just from talking to him. It helped me feel myself, the part of me I like – and that made me feel stronger.

But when I met up with Anik again, I felt the judgement come back. I felt pathetic, sick. Later, when Anik made plans to meet her French friend who lives in Avignon, I opted to spend some time on my own. See if I can scrape up some dignity. Where's that guy with the hash? Ha Ha. I made the mature decision of coming to the station instead. I'm on my third drink...

I just called home and spent $25 to talk for two minutes at a time before being cut off and having to call back. Frustrating, but probably better considering my emotional state.

By the time Anik met me in the restaurant, I was drunk and enjoying the company of Amet (the station security guard from Morocco), and Karlin (a female mechanic from Belgium). I had a great time talking with them. Karlin was so funny, complaining about working too hard to have a boyfriend and missing it majorly. She soaked up Amet's attention. I found him to be sweet and honest. He made a lot of jokes about marrying me and wanting a visa for Canada. When we parted he tried to kiss me, but was polite when denied. Anik teased me about him and being drunk. I was in a good mood and she was glad. She'd had a good time with her friend as well. We boarded the train at 1:45 am and I passed out immediately.

June 18

Off the train in Port Bou at 5:30 am, feeling pretty rough. We boarded a train for Barcelona at 5:55 am, but there was nowhere to sleep so I did the head bob thing until we got off. God, only 9:30 in the morning and I already felt like I'd had a long day. We assumed the hostels would be full, and no point in racing the 150 backpacks that got off the train with us. No problem, we found a great room in a pension with a shower/tub, double bed, and large French doors opening onto a balcony. It overlooked an alley that seemed to be under construction but hey, can't have everything. Besides, it was a relief to get the packs off.

We walked all over the city, soaking in our first glimpse of Spain. It's great! The people are so friendly and alive. They smile and make a real effort to communicate when you need help. They seem so energetic and passionate. I like this city. I like the plants and laundry hanging everywhere. The cathedral is beautiful. Apparently the construction all over the place is for the 1992 Olympics. The problem with the construction, aside from the noise, is the dust – cough...

We did that "walk for hours looking for food until I had a headache" thing again. But it was a great day. Anik was in a funny mood. Lots of laughing, hitting and side-kicking each other. Fun. I'm going to bug her FOREVER about looking up at the HUGE (later identified as Christopher Columbus) monument and, in response to the question, "Who is that?") saying, "He must have been important." Ya think so?

Near the start of our food hunt, we went into a pizzeria, saw meat hanging from the ceiling with flies all over it, and did an about face. Hours later, where do we end up having dinner? The hanging meat decor seems to be quite common and this place had good prices. We had a delicious Lasagne ($5) with a huge bottle of wine ($3). I ran out and bought a pack of Marlboro because the cheap Spanish ones Anik talked me into were gross. She quit smoking months ago, but claimed to be a good judge of a fine cigarette. Ya? Don't quit your day job.

By the end of the wine, we had a good buzz on, Anik was smoking the gross cigs, and we were talking about her running from emotion and commitment in relationships – keeping safe. Just a guess of course, but she was very interested, agreeing, and asking if I was a witch. We bought two bottles of wine for $1.90 each and went back to our room.

We sat on the floor by the open balcony door, each drinking out of our own bottle, smoking and talking. We talked about partying, drug abuse, and death. Anik talked more about losing her father, the friend she saw drown, and a suicide she witnessed as a teen. She thought these experiences with death might be the source of her fear of commitment. As we talked, getting drunker by the minute, she became very upset. She told me about suicide attempts in the past, cocaine abuse, etc. It was hard to believe this strong, assertive woman ever had such moments of doubt.

    We eventually came to talking about our connection, and her leaving. She came to Barcelona to say good-bye. She has her dream of Europe to fulfill, and was losing focus by focusing on me. I heard myself telling her how I feel – that I want to be with her, that I love her, and that I know she feels the same way. Otherwise, she wouldn't find it so draining, and it wouldn't be so hard to say good-bye. Today, and every day we've been together, we're connected as if with a string as we walk the streets of these cities. We're constantly looking at each other, seeing how the other is reacting to something, seeing how the other feels, making sure the other is still there. Whether our eyes meet across museums, or merely inches of space, it fills us with joy. I've seen it happen to her. I would never have had the courage to tell her how I feel if I hadn't.

    I surprised myself with this admission, but something had shifted during the conversation. I saw that Anik is as troubled as I am about her feelings for me! My shame lifted like fog with that realization, and left me feeling strong and certain and happy. Weird as it all is – we are in this together! And when it isn't weird – it is incredible! Unfortunately, she didn't share my relief. She didn't want to talk about it at all, and would only say that we had to go our own ways soon – hard or not. She was silent after that and a gloom fell over the room.

    I cried into the bottom of my wine bottle for the loss that was coming. She finally said it was time to sleep and crawled into bed. I got in and she pulled me to her. Holding me tight, comforting, caressing, looking into my eyes. She pulled me into a deep kiss and we fell into each other. I've never kissed anyone like that before, never felt so right in someone's arms. She spoke passionately in French, and it sent shivers through my body. She was strong and gentle.

God, it was the most passionate experience of my life. I guess I finally fell into a deep and contented sleep.

June 19

I woke up at 3 am with my contacts still in. God I hate that. Woke up again at 6:30, hungover as hell. Anik woke up and said it was late. I laughed and told her it was only 6:30. We cuddled and kissed and looked into each other's eyes as we touched each other's faces. Tracing. Loving. It was beautiful. I've never been more comfortable, relaxed, able to look into someone's eyes for so long without looking away. Our love filled the room.

Up and showered and off to the hostel since we booked and paid for it yesterday. Anik was very ill. She was in the bathroom a lot and when we walked to the hostel she was bent over and dragging herself. I couldn't help but laugh. Could it have been that top-of-the-line wine? Chablis de disinfectant 1990... We left our packs at the hostel and walked back to the Rambles. Chocolate ice cream and a hamburger for breakfast, and then, feeling very ill, headed for the beach. All the while we walked, we laughed to ourselves and each other about last night. How did it happen? Neither of us knew. She wanted to know why. I didn't really care.

On the beach, we relaxed for a while and then came to talk about it. She said her answer was partly alcohol, and partly love for me, and that she would leave for France tomorrow. We talked it inside out and I finally decided to give up and go to the train station to plan my trip, alone, to Madrid. She became upset that I didn't ask her to come too. So we walked together. I told her that my instincts told me that she felt the same way I did and she was running. She said I was wrong, but I couldn't accept it. Her leaving – yes. That she felt a need to run – yes. That she didn't feel the same way – no.

At dinner she was quiet. It bothered her that I would see her as a runner. As we ate, the sadness came and went like waves washing over me. I wanted to enjoy our last night together but as we looked into each other's eyes across the table I was reminded that

I might never see those eyes again. Her smile. Her laugh. The way she talks. Passionate French whispers in the night. The feel of her skin next to mine. I've never felt this way in my life. I wanted her to change her mind.

At the same time, I wanted to set her free. I wanted her to be happy. I felt no blame or anger or rejection – only loss, sadness. I knew she loved me, so only sadness. She took my picture across the table. We walked to the beach. It was quiet. We listened to the sound of the sea. We talked a little. She gave me a stone – "The nicest one in Barcelona". Then she said she wished we were still at the pension. She said this morning was beautiful and she'd like to spend the night without other people, talking, alone.

My mind started going. Hope. If I suggested moving from the hostel, would she reject the idea, and could I handle that disappointment? I took a chance. She was surprised and thought long and hard on it on the way back to the hostel. I felt good. I knew it didn't matter what she answered. I put it out – walked through the fear. She felt sick all of a sudden, stomach cramps and headache. She said she knew it was psychosomatic. I beamed. I knew what it meant. My instincts were right. So she said okay and we left with our packs. We were crazy and we both knew it and laughed. On the way, I started to get nervous. I think she was too. We ended up going to a nice hotel because our place was full. We got a room with a balcony overlooking the Rambles. We had showers and sat on the balcony. I was soooo nervous.

After a short silence, we admitted our nervousness and it washed away. She spoke of her discomfort of being with a woman for the first time. Doesn't understand it. I couldn't speak about my own confusion. It was too painful for me to go there. So I just listened and nodded and smiled compassion at her. All that mattered to me in that moment was that she was there. We curled up like perfectly matched spoons and went to sleep. "We fit" is the last thought I remember.

Denial isn't a river in Egypt

June 20

I AWOKE HAPPY AND sad. The day to say good-bye. It made me feel tired and sick. We finally took showers to go down for breakfast. It was lousy and neither of us felt very well. Anik suggested we get another room and sleep all day and night for a good start tomorrow. I grinned, suddenly feeling a lot better. We got our old room back at the pension. It was like coming home. We crawled into bed and spent the day talking and sharing our love through our eyes, our mouths, and our touch. She said she loved to kiss me. I'd never kissed anyone so much, and it was heaven. I was experiencing passion for the first time.

While Anik was asleep, I sat on the balcony and smoked, remembering a dream I had long ago: in a bed in a strange place, a petite woman with brown hair, and the serene feeling of being loved. The woman went out to get food and I watched through the window as she disappeared down the street. I can remember the dream and the extraordinary feeling well. I'd tried to fall back to sleep and continue, because it had felt so good. I looked over at Anik sleeping in the bed, and I knew this was that dream.

When she woke up, we went out for lunch – lasagne and wine of course. We talked about movies, jobs, and Shirley MacLaine. We have so many common interests it's amazing – we can just talk and talk. She's a movie nut like me and has been telling me about some great foreign films she's seen. I'll have to write them down so I don't forget. She also really likes Woody Allen and says I have to see "Hannah and Her Sisters". Her favourite movie is "The Big Blue" about a guy who relates to dolphins. She says it's a touching story with a great soundtrack.

I told her about the Transformational Therapist training course and some of the wild things that happened in it. I didn't get into all my issue stuff, just some of the regressions like when Tom was there and that band of light went across the room from me to him. It's easy to talk to her about that stuff. I don't feel like she'll think I'm odd or anything. She's really curious about it.

When we got back to the room, we got back into bed and the warmth of each other's arms again. God, it's so good between us. Don't judge it Riley; enjoy it. It's too beautiful to be wrong.

She held me close, gently brushing the hair off my face with her hand and kissed my forehead. As I drifted off to sleep, she whispered softly, "Dream of angels, dream of me." And I think I did….

We slept for a couple of hours and then talked in bed for a while. She wanted to know more about the regressions. I explained how I'd identified with the life of someone, in a regression, that had been killed after trusting in her inner voice and acting on it. In the regression, I was her – dying, afraid, angry, betrayed – but the feelings I experienced in the regression must have been mine. They were familiar.

Suddenly, Anik stopped me and said, "In your regression, you were Jeanne D'Arc" (Joan of Arc's real name in French). "Whoa" she said, mopping her brow, as I smiled in astonishment. I asked her how she'd guessed and she said a picture just came into her mind. Barely acknowledging how weird *that* was, I told her about the regression, my inability to process the emotions that arose – and my frustration now, at not being able to remember anything.

We went to McDonald's to eat (punishment for our sins). Anik kept laughing nervously and said she had a headache and felt ill (even before she ate). She was nervous and jumpy and anxious to leave. We returned to the room and bed. I was curious about her reaction and I felt very strange. Not about telling her, just strange. She looked at me for a long time with a very serious expression and then suddenly turned away. She became upset and would only say that another picture had come into her mind – something bad. I knew somehow, suddenly, that this had something to do with her. She had been there. She had seen the death. Who was she? My head ached and felt strange and heavy. Who was she? I tried to picture her there, to know who she was. I couldn't. I also knew this had something to do with her experience of death in this life – watching people die. And these last 13 days – the strength of our connection, her running, trying to fight her love for me. It had something to do with this too. Whoa. The pieces started to fall together quickly – too quickly. I tried to clear my mind and ask who she was.

Through this silence I knew she knew she was there. I wanted to help her. She had her back to me and I said, "I think you were there." Without turning over she said, "I think I killed you." We were silent for a long time. "Is it possible?" she said finally, turning to me. I said, "Yes, it's possible." If I've learned anything in the past two years, it's that anything is possible. Life is more than we can see with our eyes, more than what we've been taught. I don't believe in coincidence anymore. There's a reason for everything, a learning opportunity, and this thing between us is… I don't know. She told me the picture she'd seen was a stake with people all around and her nephew was there. She was very scared and said she had been since she'd first realized who I was. I tried to explain that I didn't believe I actually was Joan of Arc – it was just a learning experience accessed through the collective unconscious or something – tapping into the energy of Joan of Arc's life somehow. "I obviously have more to learn from it," I thought, a familiar dread stirring in the pit of my stomach.

Then Anik was above me, kissing me, looking into my eyes. She was Anik and I felt her love – AND THEN SUDDENLY HER FACE CHANGED!! It was someone else with cold dark eyes and sharper features. It scared me more than I've ever been scared in my life. I felt cold and it was hard to breathe. I turned immediately away, shaking, gasping. I couldn't look back. I was terrified and my mind screamed. "Holy shit – I'm going crazy." I wouldn't face her until she turned on the bright overhead light. Then I looked at her, still scared, afraid to see that face again. She asked me what happened. She was scared too. She'd seen the fear in my eyes when I jumped, and knew I was still scared. I relaxed a little into her embrace and we comforted each other. But for the rest of the night I kept thinking I'd see it again, and I felt afraid. I was afraid to sleep.

Like something would happen to me...ridiculous, crazy, but I couldn't shake it. I lay awake a long time after she fell asleep, looking into the dark and wondering what the hell was going on.

June 21

I dreamt of a man, massive and strong, who was hurting women. Only I knew it was him. A woman with children was going to be alone and I knew he'd go after her. The children were off somewhere and she was vulnerable, weak. For some reason, I couldn't tell anyone about him. I was walking, and he was coming toward me. I could see him over the hedge. He didn't see me and I knew if he did, he'd know I knew about him and he'd hurt me. I was so scared as I carefully sidestepped around the hedge, holding my breath. I was acutely aware of his power, his evil, and my fear of him. I woke up in a sweat.

I wanted Anik to change her mind about separating, but she said she couldn't. She had her answer: we knew why we'd been drawn together and now we had to go on alone and work it through. I knew she was right about this part; I know I have something to work through on my own, but I can't believe we, Riley and Anik, are done. I can't accept that. I don't want to give her up. I love her.

I was sitting in a chair, moping, when I leaned over and picked up Anik's "Let's Go Europe" book and opened it randomly. It opened on France. I turned one page and there it was: "Maison du Jeanne D'arc" (in Orlean). I slammed the book shut. Jesus. I guess I'm ready. I quickly packed up my things, my path now laid out before me. I still felt heavy with sorrow, but a calm fell over me – a resolve and confidence.

On the way to the station, I told Anik that I was going to Orlean instead of Madrid. She was shocked. She had been behind me when I opened the book. "Why, what did you find there?" Before I answered, she set her backpack on the sidewalk and pulled out the book to see what I had read about Orlean. Seconds later, she dropped it on top of her pack and walked back the way we had come. I just watched her; I knew she was upset. She stopped after a block and just stood there for a few minutes. She was laughing when she came back. "You're a witch" she teased.

"No I'm not."

"Witch."

"I'm not. I guess it's just time. I guess I'm ready to go and see."

"You're a witch."

"Shuddup, I'm not."

At the train station, we talked over tea. She told me she'd looked in the ticket office and I wasn't there and so she thought I'd just left her without a word. She was upset. I reassured her. I told her I wanted her to come with me. Do it together. She said she couldn't. She wanted a book to read and think on it before going back into France (she'd got a ticket for Italy). I understand how she feels. She's overwhelmed and scared. It's all too weird, too much at once. I also know I have to do this alone. I have something to learn from Joan. And it's about everything somehow. I feel like my trip has been building up to this moment. All that fear in the beginning, the strange dreams, Jamie and I going our separate ways, meeting Anik, losing my bike, seeing the flames in that church in Vienna, remembering Joan (but oddly nothing about her), these feelings for Anik. It's all connected. It's all meant to be. No coincidences.

We were booked on the same train to Cerbere, where we'd have a few hours together before catching trains that would carry us far from each other. While we were waiting, I opened her book randomly again. This time it opened at "Rouen" and Joan of Arc's name once again caught my eye. I read, "She met her maker at the stake..." I dropped the book. My body reacted violently. I went cold instantly and was moving across the station, feeling a need to run, to escape. I felt like I was going crazy. Maybe I am.

I walked back to show Anik, who sat slumped in her chair looking at me with a strange smile on her face. "Now what?" she asked hesitantly, probably not wanting to know. She read the passage, dropped the book, and walked clear across the station. I couldn't help but laugh. I laughed hard in fact, and it felt good. When she came back, she asked me what I was going to do. "I guess I'm going to Rouen after Orlean." What else can I do?

Anik was quiet on the train, distant and upset. She'd look at me long and hard, and then stare out the window again or close her eyes. Not once did she look at me that I didn't feel her love. We didn't want to part, but we knew it had to be – at least for now. She got another picture in her mind but wouldn't tell me what it was. At one point she looked at me, pain in her eyes, and said, "How can I accept that I might have killed someone, even if it was in another life?" I told her that I didn't believe it was her, not who she is now anyway. It may have been her, once, maybe not, but the most important thing is that she is identifying with that lifetime, that incident, for some reason. It must be an opportunity to heal something that affects her life now. She has to focus on that, but I know how overwhelming it is. I remember well being in those confusing shoes.

In Cerbere, I booked a bed on the 20:45 train to Orlean. She wasn't coming with me, and though I knew I probably wouldn't be able to sleep, I wanted to hide away from people. I knew I was going to feel awful and that the tears would not be held down.

Over dinner, I tried to reassure Anik. I told her what I'd learned from my regressions – how I came to believe that we have to walk in a lot of different shoes on our journey toward wholeness. I believe we have forgotten who we are, and live our lives disconnected from our true selves, our powerful spirit. I told her about "No Boundary" and that owning back the parts of ourselves that have become shadows are steps toward consciousness, waking up from the dream we call life. Also, that I believe all this craziness is the universe working with us to create a learning opportunity toward healing, toward our return to that whole. Any opportunities to let go of judgement, to forgive others, to have compassion, take us there...

We sat on the beach and watched the waves for a while. I started to cry. She gave me another stone, "The most beautiful in France." I laughed through my tears. Her eyes broke my heart – seeing her pain, her love. She said it had never been so hard to say good-bye. We talked about Vancouver/Quebec – I said I'd come. I'd find a way.

She's going home to start a master's degree. I'll go home broke. But I'll find a way.

She was planning to take the same train as me and transfer at Narbonne. She asked me to promise that if she couldn't get off, that I'd make her. She was afraid of waking up in Orlean, of not being able to leave me. I said I couldn't promise that and if she ended up there it would be right. She said then she'd stay in Cerbere until the 23:05 train. She had to. God it hurt. Now I had to say good-bye in half an hour. Why? It crossed my mind that it was right for me to go to Orlean feeling this way. Yes, it was right. I was scared about Orlean and Rouen. Not sure what I was doing. Afraid I'd find no answer. Afraid I would. Am I just crazy? Afraid of that too...

We walked to the station. On the platform, facing her, I found I couldn't cry. We looked at each other for a long time. She cried for the first time. We wished each other answers and good trips. We told each other I love you. She asked me to push her from my mind and not lose a day of my trip to it. I told her I wouldn't push her out. We hugged and I boarded the train. I stopped and watched her walk away. She turned and saw me and then kept walking. I put my pack in my room and went back to the door. So much emotion. I didn't know what to do with myself. I wanted to run after her, but I couldn't. I stood and looked through the window. She came back and our eyes met. God. I sat in the open door and she stood before me, looking into my eyes, smiling, loving me. I said I still wanted her to change her mind. She said, "I can't." I said, "I know," and the tears came again. "I know. I know. I love you."

"I love you too."

"I know."

She held my hands and we looked at each other. She said, "I hope I see you again." I said, "You will." If she said anything more I don't remember. She let go of my hands and walked away. I sat there and cried. My chest heaved and I shook inside. I stared ahead until the door closed automatically and I had to jump out of the way. I stood and looked out the window, wanting to catch another glimpse of her. She was there. Standing there. We just looked at each other through the window as the train pulled away. I smiled and half waved, not taking my eyes from hers. When she was out of sight, my head screamed, "Stop the train, it's a mistake, somebody stop the bloody train." I stared out the window at scenery that had no meaning. I could see the reflection of my eyes in the glass, red and full of pain.

I took my contacts out and crawled into bed at 9 pm. I lay there for an hour and a half, thinking of her, images filling my mind. It was unbearably hot and I could hardly breathe. I walked to a seat cabin and smoked. I felt awful. I wanted her with me. Why? Why? I went back to bed and lay awake for a long time.

June 22

I woke up at 6 am, surprised that I'd slept at all. Dozed until 6:30, feeling the sadness come back like a heavy coat. Got off the train in Orlean at 7 am, walked into a coffee shop and opened my journal to find this quote by Martin Buber on the top of the page, "All journeys have secret destinations of which the traveler is unaware." So I closed it. Enough already.

At eight I took a tour into nowhere and ended up outside of Orlean. Great. The wind was strong and cold. I tucked my head down and plodded on, determined to move forward. I eventually found tourist info and got a bus to the hostel, which is closed until 5:30 pm. Now I'm in a laundromat and I've been sitting here for 4 hours – writing, thinking, brooding. It's time to move on to whatever my day holds – hopefully with a clear head, if that's possible. Not really, but I feel more ready, though reluctant, to take more in. I'm scared – but now I'm going.

Well I survived. I went first to the Maison Du Jeanne D'Arc, feeling very nervous. The original house was destroyed in the war and was reconstructed. She just stayed here during the battle of Orlean. She was quite the girl, only seventeen years old, when she led an army into a successful battle that released Orlean from a 7-month siege by the English. She received an arrow in the chest during this battle.

The only mention of the voices was that some of the English were scared by her firm announcements in battle that she was led by God. Everything else – books, display, videos, were in French. I needed an English book. I went next to the Centre du Jeanne D'Arc, which turned out to be a research centre for Joan of Arc history (part of the college).

The staff were very nice and pointed out a number of English books that I could sit and read. I picked two – one about the whole story, and one about the trial. I opened one to a picture of a man AND LOOKED INTO THE COLD DARK EYES I'D SEEN IN ANIK'S FACE. NO FREAKIN WAY! THIS IS REAL LIFE NOT THE TWILIGHT ZONE!! I closed the book and started to get up to leave but when I looked around the room, the atmosphere was so normal, I sat down again. Maybe I'd imagined it. I've been very emotional lately... so I looked at the picture again expecting... but nope, it was him – the face I'd seen. I reminded myself to breathe.

The man in the picture turned out to be Pierre Cauchon, a French Bishop under the King of England, Henry VI, who was a baby at the time. Cauchon was responsible for bringing Joan to trial, for leading the inquiry, for reading the death sentence at the trial and at the stake. Too damn freaky...

Cauchon took her from the Burgundians, who'd captured her, to castle Rouen and imprisoned her. The authors of both books described him as a wicked man, and the controlling factor in the outcome. He was thought to have had personal hostility toward her because her success had somehow driven him from his Diocese the year before? I wish Anik were here to share all this. I'd like to know if it means anything to her.

On the way back to the hostel, I stopped at the statue of Joan, noting how small she was and thought of Anik. "I'm tall" she'd insisted. "Not on my side of the country," I told her. "Well I'm tall in Quebec," she replied snottily. In other words, "piss off and don't bug me about it". Ya right. I looked at the statue's face. "Who were you Jeanne D'Arc and what do you have to teach me?" I thought of what she'd accomplished. She fought for the independence of

France from England. She inspired the French spirit, which helped them win that independence. I thought of Anik and her desire for Quebec's separation from English Canada. I miss that little French woman so much. It's such a terrible feeling.

I decided to move on to Rouen right away. There was nothing more for me to do in Orlean, and I wanted to keep going. I'd like to read her statements at the trial. I ate and hopped a train to Paris, falling asleep on the way. So tired... I woke up when we arrived in Paris and fell into the chaos of the main train station. What a nightmare! Then add subway stress to another station to get my connection to Rouen! I thought about Anik on the 90-minute ride – wondering where she was, what she was doing – wishing I'd arrive in Rouen and she'd be there, waiting for me. It wasn't going to happen, but god I wanted it.

I arrived in Rouen and was able to find the youth hostel with no problems. The girls in my room are very nice, two from North Carolina and one from Boston.

I wanted to explore my interest in Joan. The statements, messages from God... War – in the name of God? Separation – in the name of God? I know that war and separation have been purposeful at times, freeing people from oppression, etc. But being led by God to kill people? to lead others to their deaths? How do Christians reconcile that contradiction? While she was a heretic at the time, she was eventually made into a saint. I tried to imagine what it must've been like for Joan – betrayed by her own people, charges of heresy, abandoned by the God that she believed had led her...

June 23

I woke up in the night to someone talking in her sleep, "You know? You know? You know?" In my head I thought, "Ya, I know," as if she was speaking to me. But I don't know a damn thing today. Nada.

I walked to the station with the girls from my room. The hostel is booked, so I'll take a night train back to Barcelona. It hurts to think of going back there, but I can't stop moving. I can't relax. I made a reservation and threw my stuff in a locker, excusing myself from the others politely. I said I had some research to do. I knew I had to be alone.

I started out at the Abbey of St. Ouen where Joan of Arc was tried. At first I got the same feeling I had looking at the other churches here. Dark and looming above me, it seemed powerful, intimidating – and intended to be that way. I sat on the grass under a tree, looking at it for a long time. I tried to imagine that day. I wanted to know what she said. I got up and walked around the outside. I thought it seemed strange that the sun was shining on me. When I reached the front door, I sat down again, facing it. She entered here. I tried to recall the feelings from my regression, or from when I saw the face in Anik's, but the sun continued to shine and a small child walked up to me and smiled. His innocence touched me. I smiled back and rose to enter the church.

Except for a man sitting quietly at a table with pamphlets, it was quite bare, unused. The few chairs in the centre of this huge, deserted church seemed… I don't know… so strange. They enhanced the emptiness somehow. I walked around, my footsteps echoing faintly, and tried to keep my mind clear so I could be in touch with my feelings, or inner guidance. One thought turned over and over in my mind – "It's dead, harmless." This thought, I realized, had started outside. I had been thinking as I walked around it, "You're just an old building." I'd also seen it in the child's smile.

It was very different from the other churches I'd visited – where there was a living energy, both of the present and the past. Here I felt nothing. I sat in one of the chairs and let my mind wander. I felt relieved. There was nothing "all-mighty" there – and there never was. This was only ever a building. I could feel my surprise, as though I had expected a monster to appear, something powerful and righteous – something I wanted to stand up to and scream at, "Oh yeah? Who the hell do you think you are? What right did you have to judge her?" But there was no monster, no powerful force of "right," no representatives of God to confuse me, condemn me… It was just a quiet old building, dust drifting in the rays of light that came through the upper windows. The only force that had ever been there were people – each with the opportunity to judge, blame, or forgive.

My regression told me that the fire that consumed Joan was a fitting symbol for the rage within her. She had been betrayed – by her church and her king. "And by her God?" I'd wondered at the time. She was sentenced to death for heresy, a cruel end for a young woman who'd believed she was acting on God's guidance... I knew it didn't matter what the truth was. It was what "I" felt, what "I" saw, that mattered today. I closed my eyes and let myself go to the images of the regression. I saw her in the flames, and then I was her, and I felt the anger grow into a rage that threatened to explode from my body – loud, violent, and toxic: "WHO ARE YOU TO JUDGE ME?" I opened my eyes to the empty church and knew with all certainty that I carried both the victim AND the monster – a cruel, unswerving judge.

I closed my eyes and turned my attention back to my body – now growing heavy with the mire – and the desire for a drink or a joint. I asked myself what the mire had to do with Joan. The answer was like a whisper in my ear, "Follow it."

I focused on the noxious feeling flowing through my body – sickening and familiar. I'd identified it long ago as shame, self-disgust, self-loathing. But I still didn't understand it. As I concentrated on the feeling, images came into my mind. I thought of Erica, an old friend from high school that I had partied with until just a few years ago. As soon as I thought of her, I realized I'd had feelings for her that I hadn't understood at the time. I remembered the butterflies in my stomach when I was near her and how much I hated Ken when he first came around. It was then that I started going into the bathrooms of bars where I was drinking with friends, and giving myself black eyes and swollen cheeks. Sometimes I had to make up stories to explain them, but usually didn't have to say a word. The dark bar kept my secret and make-up took over the next day. My stomach lurched at the memory. I had never thought about what I was doing. How could I have been so blind to myself? How could I hurt myself and not ask myself why – even after all these years? I felt like I might throw up so I left the church. I was sweating and my heart was beating too fast.

I sat down on the grass and looked around. I felt better out in the sun – it was less surreal. But more images came, a violent rush of memories and realization – friends that I'd agonized over, lay beside, feeling every brush of their skin, the warmth of their bodies... How many times did I fool myself about my feelings? So many signs of confusion and pain: the alcohol and drug abuse; headaches and stomach problems; self-injury and suicidal thoughts – and the mire! I suddenly understood the shame and self-hatred that lurks in the dark corners of my mind, the fear that shows up in my dreams, the need to please and be perfect, the desire to run far away to some place I can feel free. The image of me punching myself in the face came to mind again... and then I threw up.

I've been living in a fog, not able to admit the truth to myself. Homosexual attractions – all the way back to Rachel Gardner in grade five! The affair with Danielle – and now Anik.

The pieces of the puzzle finally in place, there was a brief moment in which everything seemed perfectly still and my mind was quiet. I felt a great sadness welling up. And then the silence was broken with a thought:

I'M GAY. AND A TOTAL IDIOT.

I'M A GAY IDIOT. GREAT!

And then I got the giggles. I couldn't help it. It all seemed so dramatic and stupid! How could I be so stupid? How could I lie to myself so well – and for so long? I suck at lying to other people. How can I be so awesome at lying to myself? How could I not see something so bloody obvious? Jamie saw it. How many other people have known or wondered? I feel like an amnesia victim, getting back pieces of my life that tell me who I am. How could I be attracted to woman after woman AND NOT THINK ABOUT THE FACT THAT I WAS ATTRACTED TO A WOMAN? How could I not stop and think, "Hey, maybe these feelings mean I'm gay?" How could I never enjoy sex with men – and not think, "Hey, maybe I'm gay"? How could I suffer so much pain, hold a knife to my wrist, give myself black eyes – and never ask, "What's going on Riley? What demons cause a beloved daughter, sister, and friend to beat her own face, to want to die?"

I didn't know what to do with the whirl of emotions that were threatening to make me puke again, so I tried to concentrate on Joan. Had I seen everything she had to teach me? Though I hadn't understood it at the time of the regression, I know now that she'd shown me my fear of judgement and betrayal, of being persecuted for who I am. A fear so great I've been living in denial. That fear has influenced what I do and who I allow myself to be. And Joan has also shown me that deep down, below the fear, I've been angry as hell about it. It's like there's a list somewhere of what's right and what's good – and what's not. And I've bought into that list – as though it contains truths rather than just opinions and swallowed dogma. I wanted to scream at that list of judgements – at everyone who believes them, "I'M NOT WRONG, I'M NOT SICK, SCREW YOU." But the anger dissipated quickly into powerlessness. Why? Because some part of me believes "the list". I believe there's something wrong with me. My life has been limited by the fact that I have believed in something "out there" that I can't control – something that can hurt me. Yet the old empty church told me that the only truth is whatever we believe. It's an empty room otherwise... Yes, people can believe I'm sick or that I'm committing a sin. They can judge me about all kinds of things – but who chooses the effect it has? They can even hurt me – but who chooses the impact? Physical hurt heals, and I get to decide the emotional effect. I'm not a child anymore. I have the experience and the maturity to choose how other people affect me. I can see that judgements are about the people who make them. I can choose not to take them on. Joan's life serves as a reminder to believe in myself, and to trust in my path. Her strength and commitment to her path are a message for a woman afraid of where her path will lead. A woman who judges herself. A woman like me.

What about this rage I'm carrying? After the regression, I knew the feelings had something to do with me, but it didn't really sink in until now. The rage is mine. While I was thinking about this, an image came to mind of Pierre Cauchon reading Joan's death sentence and I felt the anger stir. It's more familiar than I'd realized. It's the same anger that arises when I see movies or news about racism, religious persecution, rape, or child abuse – anything with an innocent victim. It's a powerful anger, a righteous anger, possibly a violent anger. I feel a strength in that anger that seems unconquerable – like I could hurl grown men into space. What a contradiction – one (huge) part of me is so afraid of my homosexuality that I've been in denial since puberty, yet another part of me is the all-powerful goddess of righteousness. What other facets of my psyche am I unaware of? Forget I asked that. I don't want to know. Gay. Really? I think I might throw up again.

Okay, so I'm gay and I judge that and I'm afraid to be judged by others and I'm possibly afraid I'm an abomination or super-freak of nature. I also hate the judges (a group to which my insecure, self-abusive, deny-the-truth self belongs) and I hate anyone who presumes power and righteousness over others (a group to which my enraged righteous self belongs). No wonder I was in denial. I'm a gay homophobe and a righteous so-and-so who hates righteous so-and so's. Thank god I'm also the person who can write this, mostly calmly, and mostly without throwing up. I like this part of me – it's like being outside myself a bit, but who I really am at the same time. It's a stronger, more grounded part than I seem to function in normally. Maybe if I could stay in this place more, I wouldn't be able to deceive myself so easily. At this point, I'm feeling pretty motivated to work on that...

Back to the realizations: I'll have to forgive myself for the self-deception. I'm quite certain that beating myself up for judging myself and being afraid of judgement will not improve my self esteem. The gay thing will be hard, but I feel incredibly brave when I think about Anik. I feel like I could face anyone with her beside me. The fact is, I would not be realizing all this, writing all this, throwing up about all this – if I wasn't completely mad about Anik. My little impetus...

How can I be free of the rage? If I think about it, I feel it grow. Will it fade if I can stop judging myself and choose not to take on the judgement of others? Surely if I want to have a peaceful life, I can't stand braced behind a defensive barrier, sword at the ready. Though it does sound appealing...

A voice in my head said it was time to go, so I left. I walked toward the View Marche where Joan was burned at the stake. I thought of the day they took her there. Was she scared? Did her faith protect her? Did she feel abandoned by her god? Was she angry?

When I arrived, I spotted the monument erected where the stake had been, but I turned away and went into the Museum de Jeanne D'Arc. It was interesting. There were a lot of displays but the best was the wax display. It was a series of scenes made up of wax figures, telling the story of her life. It was narrated in French and English. It started with her at 13, when she first heard the voices, and went to her capture and death. Throughout, I heard her strength, determination, and total acceptance of her role as guided by her God. I could see how this would cause the English distress. How could they accept that God would turn against them and give victory to the French? That's probably why she was seen as a heretic. The church also couldn't condone her claims, as it would affect the faith of the people – essential to the power of the church.

In the dramatization, Pierre Cauchon is definitely the bad guy. My anger returned instantly, blaming him. But looking at him also gave me the same feeling from that night with Anik – fear. It was his eyes.

Finally, I came to the scene where she was being taken to the View Marche in a cart. The narration said that she told Cauchon, "I die today because of you."

When I heard this, I thought "No, that's wrong."

"But it's true" I told myself, "How can it be wrong?"

I looked at the figure and listened again to her accusation. The blame seemed to weaken her. It made her smaller. I wanted her to be strong, to have faith.

"She's on fire for Pete's sake – and it's that asshole's fault!"

"He thinks he's serving God."

"But he's murdering a 19-year-old girl because she believes God wanted her to help free her people – in their own damn country!"

"Okay, it is his fault – but it's God's fault too! He's letting her die."

"But you don't believe in God."

"Right... I don't. Not a deity anyway."

"So what then? Who's responsible for her death?"

"Cauchon, the church, the English who wanted her out of the way – and destiny."

"Destiny?"

I looked at Joan's young face. "They killed her, but it was also her path."

I felt my strength return with this decision, as well as the awareness of why I was really there. Joan's life has already been lived. She made her choices and faced the consequences courageously. She didn't sit home blaming the English. She fought for freedom. She risked her life for that freedom, including the freedom to claim a connection with God. She was an incredibly brave young woman.

Yes, she was judged and she paid a terrible price for following her heart, but would she have done it differently? Probably not. She probably would have fought even harder. And I can fight too – by chucking out "the list" – accepting myself for who I am (and who I'm not), and giving up the watch for the judges out there. I'm not perfect, but there's nothing "wrong" with me. No one can claim to know for certain what God is, never mind what he or she (or it) thinks – or if it thinks at all. Do I think I'll be judged for loving a woman? Yes, but by people, not a malevolent God. And though I could be shunned or beaten, I'm not going to end up tied to a burning stake.

I left the museum feeling peaceful yet serious. My insights had left me with a duty to myself. One that I know I have to hold to, scary or not. It's time to embrace my path.

Outside at the monument, I sat and ate my sandwich, watching the people go by. A statue of Joan was beside me, of her standing in the flames. A Japanese man came, knelt and kissed the ground in front of it, stood, bowed, and left. I was moved by his gesture, but wondered if his respect was for her courage to follow her heart or because he thought that she was closer to God than he. I hoped, for him, that it was the former.

I walked toward the station, thinking of Anik. I realized that the Joan of Arc experience with Anik didn't *explain* our connection. It arose *because of* our connection. It was triggered by the fears that our love brought up for us. For Anik, it seems to be about death. For me, the fear of judgement and persecution. My regression was an opportunity for me to identify with someone courageous – while at the same time recognizing the destructive emotions I have bottled up inside (and why). But I wasn't ready then. It took loving Anik to bring it all up to the surface – and give me the strength to face it. So here I am, ready to face the world with her – and she's gone. Being apart would be such a different experience if I knew I'd see her again – soon. But I'm afraid it will be a long time and that she'll push me out of her heart. But hey – if Joan's death was part of her path, then so is whatever happens to me. You can't always get what you want... As I'm writing this I'm thinking, "I hope Anik is what I need." I miss her terribly. Well you won't see her for a while, accept it. I can't. You have to. I don't want to! But you have no choice – you have no idea where she is. I'm screwed, aren't I? Okay – take a deep breath. Trust.

On the way to the station, I bumped into Sunny, the woman from Boston, so we took a train into Paris together and hung out. She's really nice, originally from Korea, living in the States for several years, on a six-week holiday by herself. We walked and walked through Paris – the Eiffel tower, Notre Dame, and so on. It was good to be with someone for a little while, but I really wanted to be alone. I felt like such bad company. I kept seeing Anik everywhere – her purple pants, her pack, her hair... but it was never her. I have to stop hoping. I eventually gave up and went to the station two hours early, tired and sad. I updated the journal, wrote a couple postcards, and got on the train to Barcelona at 9:45 pm. I went straight to bed, feeling worse by the minute as I thought about going back to Barcelona and through Cerbere.

June 24

I woke up early but really tired. Emotions are so exhausting. I'd just finished washing up when we stopped in Cerbere. I wanted to go look, but didn't let myself. She wouldn't be there. My eyes filled with tears, but I forced them back. It's too early to start the day this way. Barcelona, God. I imagine going to the pension without her and my chest becomes heavy.

I switched trains at Port Bou and tried to breathe in a new attitude with the fresh air. I have to stop this constant hoping that she'll be somewhere. I want to go find her, but I can't. I have to respect her choice and accept that somehow it's best for me too. She won't be there Riley. ACCEPT IT and move on. But why? Why does it feel so wrong? Here we are pulling into Barcelona and it hurts as much as it did the day we said good-bye...

I got off the train and went up the escalator to the terminal. Slow. No reason to hurry and I didn't know what I was going to do. Stay in Barcelona? Could I bare it? Madrid? I just didn't know. As I walked away from the escalator someone touched me on the shoulder. I turned around and there she was. Standing there. Looking at me. She said something but I only saw her mouth move. My vision felt blurry, like a dream. I felt light headed, almost faint. Emotion flooded my body. It didn't seem real, couldn't be real. I couldn't believe what my eyes were seeing. My brain couldn't accept. I'm sure only seconds passed before I reacted, hugged her, but it felt like I was frozen in time. I felt so strange. There are no words to truly describe how I felt in that moment, but from somewhere inside grew a very definite feeling - relief - thank god, the pain was over.

We went into a coffee shop and I listened to her talk about phoning the hostels in Orlean and Rouen, and when she couldn't find me somehow knowing I'd be coming to Barcelona today. She'd only arrived 20 minutes before me. Only 20 minutes! I listened to her talk and I heard her love. She really loves me. I don't know why but I don't care. I'll accept, without question, this astounding gift.

She asked me if I was sure this is what I wanted. Funny. I've never wanted anything so much in my life.

We got a great room on the Rambles for $12 each, not far from our other room, which was full. It was sooo good to hold her again. I missed her eyes and the way I feel with her. She wants to stay with me until I meet Jo and Jamie in Lisbon on July 7. She wants us to prepare together for that separation. I think I'll just take it day by day. I don't want to think about it too much and ruin this time together. I'm scared, but I don't care. She asked me to marry her and laughed. I said I would. She said, "Do you want to get married in Portugal?" I laughed back and said "Maybe," remembering the dream I had in Ireland – that I'd gotten married in Portugal and gone home early. Weird.

Over dinner (What? Lasagne again?), I told her about Orlean and Rouen. It wasn't the best place to discuss it. The new restaurant we tried wasn't great and the waiter was a jerk. Anik had mosquitoes (doing a marvellous synchronized swimming routine) in her wine. But she was interested – especially about Pierre Cauchon. It was different talking about it this time. The intensity around it was gone, the fear, the mystery. It didn't seem to be about "us" anymore. I don't know exactly what it has to do with Anik, but it's clear what it has to do with me and I don't really feel like talking about that. I want to hold the experience and insights close to me, like a talisman, warding off the thoughts that make me insecure. Loving Anik is my path now. I'm conscious of the ramifications and that scares the crap out of me, but the alternative is worse. My inner voice tells me that this is right, this is what I have to do, who I have to be right now.

We spent the evening sitting on our balcony, watching a Spanish woman sing in the street while some other women danced. It was romantic and I can't remember being happier.

Things are much friendlier with two
PIGLET

June 25

IT WAS GOOD TO wake up and find Anik still beside me – it wasn't a dream after all...

On the long train ride to Valencia I had time to think. I acknowledged the fear that has kicked in since the penny dropped in Rouen, but I'm not going to let my insecurities spoil this time for me. I can't think about the future, just here and now. I have to be myself, express my feelings, and accept Aniks. I still can't believe she's back. I can't believe she found me.

Valencia is a nice city. After finding a room, we walked and walked. We found a beautiful, old cathedral. It was covered in white birds – covered! Yet, there wasn't a single bird on any of the surrounding buildings. It was peaceful and quiet there. Anik and I were the only people and we were quiet too, listening to the soft fluttering of wings.

God it's hot here. I got dehydrated and felt dizzy. Must be hell to cycle through these hot countries. We found a good restaurant for dinner, after much looking of course. We drank two bottles of wine and talked about poetry, soccer, unconditional love, sex, and several other subjects I've forgotten.

June 26

We decided to stay another night and take a day trip to see some ruins. Delicious chocolate croissants and lots n' lots of water for breakfast. I loved the sleepy little town of Sagunto and the Roman theatre was fascinating. We wandered through the tunnels behind the seating area, looking into the cells and imagining the times – the judgement, the violence. It was a little creepy, but exciting at the same time. I couldn't believe I was in Spain, wandering around an ancient Roman theatre! And when this beautiful little French woman grabbed me and kissed me in one of the dark tunnels... Woo.

When we came out of the tunnels and into the arena, some workers had arrived and they started shouting and waving us away. I guess we weren't supposed to be there and when I stopped to take a picture, one guy came after me, waving and shouting angrily.

We realized later that the reason the town was so quiet was because it was siesta time. Here we were, wandering around in the scorching heat of the mid-day sun while everyone else was napping. Blazing or not, I loved Sagunto – calm, quiet, and peaceful. A reflection of how I'm feeling today (mostly).

While we were having dinner Anik told me her nerves are bad, that she's feeling impatient and having a hard time holding it in. I suggested she take some time to herself. I don't know what's up, but hopefully the space helped.

Later in the evening, we were making love and then Anik stopped and asked me what was wrong. I insisted nothing was. She said that we weren't making love. She felt like we were just having sex, because it was so separate. She said I wasn't even there. I started to cry. I cried for my confusing and painful past, and I cried because here was this amazing woman who loved me and really wanted to "share" her love with me. She was the first person I'd slept with to notice I wasn't really there. I hadn't noticed myself, but when she said it, I knew she was right. Then I suddenly felt stupid, embarrassed, because I didn't know what I had to offer. I had no experience making love. Sex has always been so uncomfortable for me, this thing I had to tolerate or be drunk for – this thing that always made me feel guilty and weird. I looked at her, at her eyes, and ached with my love for her... but I didn't know what to do with it.

We talked for a while and I relaxed. Then we started making love again. Together this time. It was tender and electric. It felt so right, not wrong or dirty. Anik showed me something wonderful today: I can be sober and present during sex, and it can be a beautiful and natural expression of my love.

June 27

I woke up at 6 am. Restless. Got dressed and went for a walk at 7. I walked for two hours, trying to leave my fear around a corner somewhere.

We caught a train to Mogente so we could spend the day in a little village off the map before transferring to Alicante. We just picked it off the train schedule, checked to make sure it wasn't in the travel guide and bought our tickets. When we arrived, I ditched my pannier bags in a bush, such a pain in the ass. We walked around the town, enjoying the curiosity of the locals. Sometimes people would peek out of their homes ahead of us, as if they'd heard we were on our way. After a while it got uncomfortable, as few were friendly, and we came to feel like we were trespassing. So we went back to the station.

The train station was really just a hut, with a couple of benches and a whole lot of flies and cockroaches, but we had a great experience. We met about 10 - 12 boys who were in Mogente for a picnic. They surrounded us and started trying out their English words. They ranged from 10 - 15 years old, and were absolutely charming. They acted out some things so we'd understand - like when we said we were from Canada, they wrapped their arms around themselves and said "Brrr." They were so comfortable with us - physically close, laughing. Frances, a small, skinny boy was particularly entertaining. When the train came I was sorry to go but it was a great good-bye. They helped us put our luggage on the train, waving and waving. It was the best part of the day. It also made me think about communication - how it's always possible if you're willing.

Alicante is a really touristy, ritzy type place. Like the Riviera, but less expensive. We found a room quickly this time, paying a little too much but it's just too hot to wander all over with our packs, looking. We went down to the beach afterward and Anik went for a swim. I was just about to join her when she came out complaining of the pollution. The price of tourism I guess.

June 28

"Good morning! Did you have a good sweat?"
"Yes I did, and you?"
"Fabulous."
Jesus it's hot here...

We were totally hyped to go to the castle this morning. The Let's Go book said there are secret passageways and tunnels. Cool. We couldn't wait to explore. What the book forgot to mention was "where?" Damn, not a secret anything to be found. In fact, most of the castle was closed off. But the view was great so I guess it was worth it.

We watched some fireworks from the beach tonight and found out that when you order a highball, you have to tell them when to stop pouring the alcohol. I watched in amazement as a bartender filled my glass 3/4 full of vodka before I said, "Zoinks" and he finally stopped.

Anik was distant today. She had a bad sleep and was out walking before I woke up. Says she doesn't want me to love her like I do, wishes she only loved me as a friend. "Too late" I said, not telling her that part of me wished the same thing.

June 29

We're in Madrid. A great room in a family-run pension. Good price, nice people. Dinner at the "Musee De Jamon" (Museum of Ham). Chocolate waffles with cream, "oops, sorry about your pants." Walked the Via Grande, the main street, which looked more like New York than what I would expect to find in Spain.

June 30

We visited the art museum "Del Prato" today and saw some incredible paintings – old, mostly religious pieces, and two that have stuck in my mind. One was of a man looking at a child on his shoulder with the world in its hands. The child looked loving, peaceful, and wise. The man looked burdened and confused. The other painting was very disturbing. It was by Reubens and called "Saturno". An old man is holding a terrified child over one arm and ripping the child's heart out with his teeth. It made my hair stand on end. Ya ya… it's like that already… but really, it gave me the creeps, the chills, the heebie jeebies. But I was drawn to it. Why would someone paint something like that? What does it mean? I wonder why, of all the paintings in the museum, these two caught my attention and stay in my mind now. They are similar in that there is a contrast between youth and age. In the first one, a contrast between a peaceful, innocent child and a troubled man. In the second, an old man taking the life of a child.

Afterwards, we went to the park for lunch and there was something else creepy. The park pond was full of the scariest bloody fish I've ever seen (aside from Jaws of course). Someone said they were just carp, but they looked like piranhas when people threw food in and they all came up at once, all over each other, mouths wide open trying to get it. The slurping sound they made will probably give me nightmares tonight. I looked at the people in boats and wondered how they could handle knowing those fish were in the water. What if the boat tipped and they fell in? I pushed the image out of my mind. What a weird afternoon. Is it just fear coming up? My heart being ripped out? Being devoured? Losing my innocence? (Did I hear someone laugh?) My stomach felt sick all afternoon. I guess facing my fears is going to be an "in progress" thing…

We got on a night train to Seville. Seville! Spent the evening sitting on the floor outside our compartment with two American women we met, Julie and Suzanne. They filled us in on all their adventures, most of which involved Julie screwing up somehow. She lost her wallet in a nightclub in Paris, got so drunk she couldn't find her hotel in Berlin, ran over some guys toes in Barcelona with the cart she uses to carry her 500 pound backpack, and so on. Suzanne told it very well and we all had a good laugh. I thought of the Larrys and wondered what they were up to...

July 1

God I had the worst sleep of my life. Did I say sleep? There was definitely no sleeping going on. It was like trying to sleep in the back of a 4x4, barrelling at 200 mph down the pot-holed road from hell. Bouncing, yes. Flying, yes. Slamming into Anik and another backpacker, yes. Getting whiplash, yes. Sleeping, no. Definitely not. I must say it was pretty funny for the first hour, but then the novelty wore off.

We got a room in a great pension by following a guy from the station. I was a little leery about it but boy am I glad we did. It's wonderful - a real Spanish house. There's a courtyard, plants everywhere, and a bird singing like nothing I've ever heard before. So romantic! We walked around the city and saw the Cathedral, which is the third largest in Europe. Then had a siesta and a nice dinner.

When Anik looks at me with those gorgeous brown eyes and says, "I so love you," I understand what it means "to melt."

July 2

We got a bus to Ayamonte, where we caught a ferry over the Portuguese border, then a train into Lagos. A lady met us on the train and asked us if we needed a room in Lagos. It sounded good, so when we arrived we followed her through the station as she pushed away other people trying to rent out rooms. The place is perfect. We have a room with two single beds, a bathroom we share with two other backpackers (a brother and sister leaving tomorrow for "The running of the bulls"), a kitchen, washer/dryer, and a balcony, which faces the gorgeous turquoise sea. All for only $8 a night!

Amazing! The woman and her husband rent out their own apartment for the summer and stay with their daughter. We've basically got the place to ourselves.

We dropped off our stuff and headed for the beach. It's a paradise. Rugged cliffs with tunnels connecting 8 beaches. The sand is full of beautiful coloured rocks and shells. Clean, blue, quiet. We sat for a long time and listened to the waves. I realized how focused I am on her. I can hardly stop talking and I want to tell her everything I think and feel. I guess this is what it's like to be in love.

We had a good dinner and then went to a pub and got bombed. We yakked and yakked and laughed. When we finally stumbled out of the bar, we realized we didn't know how to find our way back to our room. We hadn't written the address down - and all the streets look the same - full of square white buildings! While we puzzled over it in the square, an Australian guy approached us and said he was lost too. In fact, there were a whole bunch of people who'd done the same thing and we were welcome to sleep on the beach with them, safety in numbers and all that. He was nice and we cracked up at our mutual predicament, but Anik was determined to find our way home. So we staggered through the streets, up hills, and around corners (stopping to kiss and leave some skin on a few stucco walls), until we, Anik actually, found our room. Me, I would've been on the beach with the other Larrys.

July 3

We ignored our hangovers and headed out for a great day of sightseeing and sunshine. We rented motorbikes and had a blast visiting different beaches and villages along the coast, grinning from ear to ear. Anik said it felt like a honeymoon. And it does... it really does.

Back at "our" apartment, Anik cooked a great dinner of rice and veggies, which we ate out on the balcony. While we were sipping our wine and enjoying the view, a flock of magnificent white birds with coloured breasts flew in a circle over our heads. They flew in perfect unison, with a grace that showed they were part of the wind. They glided and turned, circling round and round until I felt dizzy with the pleasure of it. A neighbour came out and told us the Portuguese name for the birds and said they're a symbol of love and that she was surprised to see them circling so close. Anik leaned over and whispered, "It's our wedding ceremony" and took my hand under the table. I looked up again, noting the symbolism of the circle (ring) and the white birds. "So it is," I said to Anik. "Unbelievable," I thought to myself, remembering again the dream in Ireland and how puzzled I'd been. I felt a little overwhelmed, but so happy, so right. It's a moment I'll never forget as long as I live. Anik and I are being guided by magic.

July 4

We went to Sagris today. Walked the awesome coastline to Cape St. Vincent, the most southwestern point of Europe. The end of the world some call it. "To the end of the world and back my love," my little French cornball crooned, extending her hand in a dramatic gesture.

It was beautiful. High wind-battered cliffs overlooking white sandy beaches etched into the rock ("Hey, are those people naked down there?"). Dark blue water as far as you can see … Anik sang "Riding tru da desert on a 'orse wid no name…" as we fought the wind and danced along the flat earth.

We hitchhiked back to Sagris with a friendly local man, and caught a bus home. Our moods started to fall during the ride, as we realized our last day had been spent. Tomorrow we go to Lisbon, where we'll go our separate ways once again. We were quiet through dinner and when we tried to make love, Anik ended up leaving the bed upset. I wasn't really there she said.

July 5

Anik's upset. Me too. I was afraid she'd leave. We tried to talk it out. I had a wall up for sure. I'm so scared. I love her so much. I don't want to lose her again. But what does it mean to commit to more?

I just skimmed back a few pages and it was so interesting to read my entry on June 28. Anik was just telling me that if I'm going to stop myself from loving her that she would leave. How perfect for me to read that entry and remember her wanting to push me away. As much as I was telling Anik last night that I wanted to continue – and I do – I was holding back and I've been judging myself for that, angry with myself for hurting her, for not being stronger, for allowing the pain to push me inside. That judgement was making things worse. I could feel it and now I felt it shift and a wall has come down. We are both just so afraid – afraid to be together and afraid to be apart. We know we'll have to be apart soon, and then we live on opposite sides of the country, and our families... oh god, our families. How are we supposed to deal with all this? But we have to. We love each other so much. We have to. So I've got to understand and accept these swings – one of us shutting off and then the other – this constant struggle with our fears. Funny that I would skim back in my journal at the exact moment I needed to read that. A reminder to trust. I have guidance.

We caught a train to Tunes – the middle of nowhere, hot, nothing to do – and 4 hours to kill! Anik wrote in her journal while I counted flies and tried not to think. When we finally arrived in Lisbon, I wished I was still sitting in that dusty old station, counting those damn flies. I was really nervous about running into Jo or Jamie – afraid Anik would leave early.

We found a nice pension near the centre and lay in bed long into the night, listening to a prostitute singing in the street below. Her voice was pretty, melodic... soothing.

July 6

We walked around a bit but we were both so upset, sad. We spent a lot of time in the room together. I love being with her. I don't want her to go. It's our last night together.

July 7

Anik got up and packed but when it was time to go, she asked if she could stay another night. God, of course! Oh I love her so much.

We went to the station so she could book a ticket for the following day. She wanted to make sure she'd leave. We bumped into Jo while we were there and she noticed my hickey right away (thanks Hon!) So here I was cornered by old eagle eyes... She had a million questions. "Did you meet someone special?" "Who is he?" "Was it a one-night stand?" "Why don't you want to talk about it?" "You can tell me". And on and on through dinner until I was sweating and twitching and red as a beet trying to lie about an experience which meant so much to me. It was so hard; I hate lying, and this was HUGE. But Anik didn't want me to tell anyone, so I respected that. Or at least tried to. Anik felt so bad watching me squirm that she finally told Jo that she was in love with me. Then we told her about how we'd found each other again and our ceremony in Lagos. I loved Anik more in this moment than I ever could've imagined.

Jo, of course, was so understanding and happy for us. It was one of the best days of my life, this sharing of our love. It allowed me to feel it more – the secret unveiled – the air fed it and it grew.

July 8

It was a long, slow walk to the station. I was hurting so much, like something was strangling my entire body from the inside. "Change your mind," I thought, "Don't go." But I didn't say it aloud. I wanted to respect her decision. She had come back to me, and I had promised to let her go when the time came. When she got on the train, I nearly ran after her. I saw myself running, shouting, going with her. But I just stood there, too empty to cry. I watched the train until it was a dot in the distance, hoping to see a little French woman jump off and come running back to where I was so sure she belonged – with me.

July 9

Still no sign of Jamie so I called home and asked mom to contact Jamie's parents and then I called back a few hours later. Turns out that Jamie's been home for a week. She sold her bike in Switzerland and packed it in. Her mom said she's fine, that she had just had enough of traveling. If I didn't feel like total crap today, I'd be pissed off that she didn't get a message to us so we wouldn't worry. Oh Jamie... I hope you're okay.

Anik, where are you now? I can't sleep without the sound of your breathing (well snoring actually) beside me...

> *To go forward is to move toward perfection.*
> *March on, and fear not the thorns, or the*
> *sharp stones on life's path.*
>
> KAHLIL GIBRAN

August 16 (I arrived in Vancouver yesterday)

AFTER ANIK LEFT, I was a mess. I couldn't think about anything else. I went back to Portugal with Jo, but the minute we arrived in Lagos, I knew what I had to do. I didn't have a clue where Anik was or whether I would find her, but I had one chance. Jo had shown us her incredible photos of Switzerland. Everything we'd missed behind the clouds. Gorgeous mountains, green valleys, picturesque villas... We both said right away that we'd go back before we left Europe. Jo recommended a particular youth hostel in Interlachen, a small town near the Oberland range. Anik told Jo she would go there and wrote the address down. I figured if I went straight there and waited, I might find her. She was planning to spend time in France... so I might. I wrote her a long letter. Telling her how much I loved her, how I wanted to spend the rest of my life with her, and that I was coming. It was about 12 pages long, but it really just said that, in a 100 different ways. I mailed it express to the hostel, praying that she'd get it if she arrived before me.

It was hard to tell Jo that I was leaving. I knew she'd be disappointed, but I just had to go. I had to. She understood. She could see how miserable I was, but yes, she was disappointed too. I felt terrible about it, but I had to go. I felt I would combust if I didn't.

I caught a train from Lagos to Lisbon, where I would have a couple hours before the next train to Madrid. I had to get my pannier bags out of a locker there and would pick up some food for the long ride. The trip from Lagos was pleasant and I felt good about my decision. At least I was doing something. I had hope. There are two things I remember about the ride to Lisbon. One was the three young Swedish men in the seats across the aisle from me. A woman sitting beside me said they were on their last vacation before entering compulsory military service. She explained that Sweden is too expensive for young people to go out drinking very often and so they come to Portugal to let loose, especially before giving up their freedom for a while.

The main reason I remember them was their comfort with each other. They were drunk and happy. They teased each other but spoke seriously about life, women, and relationships. They were so sensitive to each other's feelings and clearly respected women. They shared insights that reflected maturity I'd never noticed in men their age. All the while they talked, they put their feet up on each other, rested their heads on each other's shoulders and demonstrated all kinds of physical gestures that had only one meaning in Canada... I was amazed that these obviously heterosexual men could be so affectionate with each other. A few hours later they were all curled up together, sound asleep. I felt a warmth toward them, like a proud mom.

The other thing I'll never forget about that trip is the delay. The train stopped at one point, in the middle of nowhere. When almost an hour had gone by and we were still sitting there, I decided to find out what was going on. It was mid-day and the heat was stifling. I walked up to the front of the train, and peered through the connecting door of the first car. Track, for as far as I could see. No engine. Just track. Hmm. I walked back to my seat and sat down, smiling. The Swedish woman asked me why we were stopped. "The engine's gone" I said, "Where do you think it went?"

"What?"

"The engine's gone."

She stood up and walked toward the front of the train. A few minutes later she came back smiling. She sat down and mopped the sweat from her forehead. "It's really hot," she said quietly. "Um-hm," I replied looking out the window at the heat waves. We started moving 3 hours later.

By the time we arrived in Lisbon I was in a panic. I barely had time to run, grab my stuff out of the locker and get to the main station. No time for food and I had to take a taxi. Fortunately, that train was also off schedule and I ended up being one of the first to board. I found an empty compartment and took a seat by the window, tossing my bags on the shelf above. By the time we pulled out, the compartment was packed with more bodies than seats. I discovered later, on the way to the loo, that people were sleeping in the aisles as well.

The people in my cabin were all really nice, backpackers from all over. We talked for hours, passing the time as best we could. It was hard to get comfortable, it was hot, and sleep was going to be a miracle. To top it off, the train somehow lost 6 hours in the night. I was too tired to even think about that one, but I was pretty pissed off about missing my connection to Barcelona. I killed some time emptying the locker I'd left my bike stuff in when Anik and I had passed through, and I went to see if my bike had shown up. It hadn't so I filled out a form and was told that I'd receive some kind of compensation by mail if it didn't turn up. Whatever, I was kind of relieved not to have to deal with it – though I did want my bike. We'd been through a lot together.

It was about 11:00 at night when we arrived in Barcelona, and my next train wasn't leaving until morning so I took a taxi to a hotel room. I was pooped, but forced myself to take a shower before bed. I think I was asleep before my head hit the pillow. I slept deeply, for the first time in days.

In the morning I felt human again, though anxious about the delays. I bought some clean t-shirts to tie me over until I could do laundry in Interlachen, and went back to the station. For some reason I don't remember the trip from Barcelona to Switzerland. I think I went straight to Geneva and caught another train to Bern, but I'm not sure. Hours and hours on trains from the south of Portugal to Switzerland in 3 days, and I didn't pull out my journal once. I was on a mission, and that was that.

On the station platform in Bern, I met a nice couple from New Orleans, Nick and Carolyn. They were headed to Interlachen too.

I've thought about them a few times since and about how they seemed to take me under their wing immediately. They were kind and parent-like, as if they sensed my distress. Maybe it was all over my face – knitted brow, dark circles under tired, sad eyes? I don't know what I looked like, and I couldn't care.

They decided to go to the same hostel so we walked there together. Carolyn asked if she could share a room with me, as her and Nick liked to take their space sometimes. I was happy for the company, and it helped me relax a bit. I checked the notice board immediately, where I found my letter to Anik. I took it and posted a note letting her know I was there.

In the morning, Carolyn and Nick invited me to join them for a day trip. We rented bicycles and rode to a lake where we could swim and relax in the sun. We talked, laughed, and dozed in the grass. It was nice. I could feel myself again. On the way back, I noticed myself smiling and the ease with which I pedaled along. I was pretty sure Anik hadn't been there yet which was good, very good. I'd stay until I was sure she wasn't coming. As I neared the entrance to the hostel, I wondered if she'd be there. Would she be happy to see me, or upset?

And there she was. I came around the corner of the driveway and she was standing right there looking at me. She'd been there about half an hour and had seen my note. She was surprised, overwhelmed, but not unhappy. She'd been trying to forget me she said, which I already knew. Anik is a door person. When she doesn't like the way something makes her feel, she closes the door. If she doesn't like the way something is going, she walks out one. I've never known anyone who can turn off their emotions like that. It worries me.

We went for a long walk and talked. I gave her my letter to read and she asked me how I could be so sure. Why did I love her like that? It wasn't hard to convince her. She loved me, scared or not. She made a confession that night too. She told me that she had been with a woman before, and had lied to me. Her voice shook as she told me about a long-term affair with a woman from her University, about how her Mom had found out and been furious with her, and how the woman had left her for a man, breaking her heart. She was so nervous as she told me the story, afraid that I would be angry because she'd lied. I was shocked but not angry. She said she didn't want to be with a woman again. The first was just a special "one-time" thing, but what did the second say about her? I knew exactly how she felt, so there was nothing to be angry about. She was telling me now. And that meant a lot.

We spent some time in Interlachen, doing day trips to Grindelwald and the Valley of the Waterfalls. It was beautiful and so great to be together again! We went up the longest chairlift in the world, hiked down to the melody of cowbells, walked inside a glacier (It was so BLUE), and saw the largest underground waterfall in the world. The pain was gone and life was moving along once again.

We traveled through France after that. Lyon, Tours, and the Loire Valley area. The chateau region was incredible. Chateau Chenonceau in particular. I took my best photo ever – of the Chateau stretched over the river. It was a romantic place and I was with my love. We also went to Mont St- Michel, another stunning structure, and yet another unsuccessful attempt at dungeon hunting. We were lucky we didn't get lost for days in that one.

From there to Paris, where we followed the soothing call of saxophones playing into the night. We splurged and went to a jazz bar, paying $8 a glass for draft beer, the cheapest thing on the menu. The bartender bought us a round before we left, happy we liked jazz.

I called home from Paris to tell Mom & Dad I'd be coming home early (just like in my dream – how weird is that?). Anik's flight from Amsterdam was only two weeks away, and my money was getting too low to go all the way south for any length of time. It meant giving up Greece, Turkey, Israel, and Egypt, but the word is that a war is starting in the gulf so I probably wouldn't get into Israel or Egypt anyway. So I decided to stay with Anik until she left and then go home myself. If I was going to move to Quebec to be with Anik, I was going to have to save. Might as well start now I figured. When I called home, Dad told me they'd received a letter from Switzerland – my bike had been found in Geneva and they would send it to Canada. Perfect!

From Paris we went to Belgium where we visited Brugge and Brussels. Brugge was pretty and we bumped into Nick and Carolyn. We went to an outdoor concert in the park with them and had a good time dancing to the blues.

In what seemed like no time, we were in Amsterdam, only a couple days from leaving each other again. On the first day, I arranged a flight, which would leave within an hour of Anik's. Though I wasn't quite ready to go home yet, I didn't feel like there was an alternative. We had both been to Amsterdam already and weren't in the "tourist" mode. We spent our time talking and anticipating our separation. We decided that I'd go to Quebec as soon as I had enough money to live on while I looked for work. Anik would be studying so it was the only option. We both knew it wouldn't be easy and that it would be a while before we'd see each other again. The difference this time was that we knew there would be a next time. We were going to make a go of it.

I don't actually remember much about Amsterdam except that we went to see "Pink Floyd – The Wall" at a theatre, after sampling the local vegetation. It was a great experience, compounded by the fact that we had the theatre to ourselves. It was the first time Anik and I smoked pot together. We'd tried in Lisbon and bought what was probably camel poo disguised as hashish, from a Moroccan guy. No wonder we got such a good deal. We were thoroughly pissed off – especially after sweating about buying it in the first place. The guy had followed me around for ages, flashing this huge chunk at me from under his shirt. I kept saying no and walking away but finally caved in (with Anik's encouragement) and wasted my money.

The night before we would fly out of Amsterdam, we went to a nice restaurant for a romantic candlelit dinner, promising ourselves we wouldn't drink or get stoned. We wanted to enjoy every moment and not waste a precious second. Ya right. From the bottle of wine at dinner, we went to beers at the Bulldog, a pub with tables overlooking an active square of street entertainers etc. At some point we bought some hash and rolled it up with tobacco.

I don't remember going back to our room but I do recall waking up beside Anik about 6:30 am, fully dressed including coat and shoes. In fact, our feet were still on the floor. I woke Anik up and stumbled to the bathroom. We had to leave for the airport in less than 30 minutes. When I came out of the bathroom Anik was really upset. We'd blown it. We had spent our last night together bombed. I tried to comfort her but it was useless. She was tired, hungover, and upset. Our time was gone.

And what a day from hell. At the Amsterdam airport, I was pulled aside and questioned for what seemed like hours. Are you traveling alone? Has anyone asked you to take something back with you? Who's that woman waiting for you? Has she had access to your luggage? And so on until I thought I'd scream. It didn't go with my hangover too well and they were taking up valuable time. Time that I wanted to spend with Anik. After going through my bags, they finally let me go. "What the "ell?" said my little grump. "Never mind, let's just enjoy this time," I replied weakly. Too much to deal with on a hangover that's for sure. Long before we were ready, we had to say our good-byes and promises – promises to write, promises to call, promises to be together again soon…

I boarded the plane hung over and exhausted, two days from home, with the frustrating inability to sleep sitting up. From Amsterdam I flew to London, where I waited in the airport for four hours. I bought a novel in the gift shop, an attempt at passing the time. But I couldn't read. My eyes were sore and my thoughts jumped all over the place. When the time finally arrived to board my flight, I was pulled out of the line-up and questioned AGAIN.

I got on the plane a little indignant, and my mood deteriorated with each of the 10 hours I spent trying to get comfortable. I hate flying. Crappy food, no sleep, cramped legs, a sore back, stiff neck, and what that air does to my sinuses ought to be grounds for a lawsuit. Fortunately, my mood shifted considerably with the announcement that we would soon be landing at the Seattle airport.

In fact, when they brought the dogs up to sniff my bags as I entered the customs area, I couldn't help but smile and look around, "Am I on Candid Camera, or what?" A much better reaction than "WHAT'S THE F...ING PROBLEM?", which I have to admit was just as likely.

I called home from Seattle after booking a flight to Vancouver. A two-hour wait, a short flight, and I'd be home. I was excited, but felt strange at the same time. I felt so different. So much had happened. I looked at myself in the bathroom mirror – I mean REALLY looked, for the first time in months. I looked tired, but good. Tanned, healthy, fit, and happy. Red as my eyes may have been, I couldn't help but think they showed what I'd been living. Love, passion, romance – me!

On the flight to Vancouver, I overheard a woman behind me telling someone about the horrible trip home she'd had. She was strip-searched in Frankfurt, questioned in London, etc. I leaned over my seat and told her that I'd been hassled as well. She said that it was because there'd been a bomb scare. The authorities had got a tip that a young Canadian woman traveling alone would board a flight from Frankfurt that day with a bomb – so they were checking all the major airports in Europe. Oh thank god I hadn't boarded in Frankfurt... My hassle seemed so minor in comparison. An extremely hungover person can only cope with so much – and a strip search is not on that list. Thank you, Universe, for sparing me the "assaulting an officer" charges.

Mom and Dad picked me up from the airport with Grandma. It was great to see them all and we immediately started yabbering about everything. Then, as Dad was pulling the car out of the airport parking lot, Mom told me that I was arriving in Vancouver at a pretty strange time. "It's the gay Olympics," she said with a laugh, "There are gay people all over the place." Her and Dad laughed and made a few more comments while Grandma just shook her head. I didn't hear what else they said because I was feeling a little sick. Did I say a little? Suddenly the reality of coming home sunk in, and I was (am) scared to death.

August 18

Today I woke up knowing I have to tell them the truth. I am in love with Anik, and they are going to find out sooner or later. So I decided to start with Mom. I knew it wouldn't be easy, but I thought the fact that I was happy would help. I was wrong.

I sat down at the kitchen table when everyone else was out and Mom was cleaning up. I said that I had something important to tell her. My voice was shaking and I felt just sick inside. I could barely look at her, my face was hot and my mouth dry. I tried to remind myself that the only judgement that can hurt me is mine. I saw Anik's eyes. How can our love be wrong? It's not. So I continued.

I said, "It's about Anik. She's more than my friend. I'm gay."

She let out a wail and dropped something. "Oh no Riley," she said, her tone ringing hurt and disappointment in my ears. My head dropped lower, and my entire body shrunk, but I tried to stay focused. "I love her and I want to be with her."

She tried to reason with me, "You're just confused about your feelings because of the great experiences you had together."

"No, it's more than that, and it's not the first time. I've been with a woman before."

"Oh my god Riley, no, no."

"Yes. I didn't want to turn out this way. I tried to be happy with men, but I couldn't."

"You just haven't met the right guy."

"Maybe, but right now I love Anik, and I've never felt this way about anyone." I tried to convince her that it wasn't just a passing thing, that I thought this was who I was, but everything I said just made it worse. I'd been crying from the beginning but it grew so I couldn't talk anymore. I am so bad at confrontation; I always end up crying and unable to stick up for myself.

I've forgotten the order of what came out after that but I'll never forget what was said: "It's against God" (except for the "freaks of nature," like when a man is born in a woman's body), "It's sick", "How old is she? I'd like to talk to her mother!" "What about Aids?" And the line I hear over and over in my mind: "If I knew you were going to turn out this way, I would've drowned you when you were born. I mean it Riley. Don't you ever EVER think I didn't mean it."

She told me that if I was going to live my life that way, that it'd be best to go somewhere else. It would kill my father and tear the family apart - and there was no way she was going to let that happen. No way. So I said I'd go away. I left the room, still crying, feeling like I'd been beaten to a pulp.

August 20

I came home late last night. The house was dark, but before I was safe inside the suite, I heard my name. It startled me and I froze, wondering if I'd imagined it. "Come up here" she said. So I dragged myself up the stairs, anger brewing beneath the weight of my sadness. She was sitting in the dark on the sofa. Her ember briefly lit her face when she took a drag, showing her disapproval, her coldness. "I've been trying to figure out what could've happened to you. You weren't like this when you were little. Did someone do something to you?"

I let out a sigh. "I'm not like this because something happened to me. People are born gay."

"Yes, but you weren't."

"How do you know?" I snapped back. "Children aren't anything. Sexuality develops later and I had feelings like that way back then, I just tried to ignore them."

We sat in the silence for a few minutes. As far as I was concerned, there was really nothing to say. I was tired. "I'm worried about you," she finally said, in that same stern tone.

"You don't have to worry about me. I'm happy."

"What will happen to you when you die?"

"What are you talking about?"

"Everyone has to face God before they enter heaven."

"I don't want to hear anymore. I'm tired, I'm going to bed." So I got up and left her, smoking in the dark.

August 21

I dreamt my clothes were on fire and woke up slapping at my bed sheets.

August 22

I called Anik at her Mom's in Quebec, after rehearsing the French she'd taught me: "Est-ce que Anik est la, s'il vous plait?" It was reassuring to hear her voice, and her love, when I was feeling so low. The distance, and the time which stood between us was discouraging, but she was there. I didn't tell her what happened and tried to sound positive. Oh how I wish we were still in Europe. It's already starting to seem so long ago.

August 24

Anik called, sounding hesitant but excited. She'd registered at the university for her master's and signed a one-year lease for an apartment yesterday – but then she went back this morning, withdrew her registration, and is trying to get out of the lease. She's coming to Vancouver!!!!!

I'm shocked but thrilled. I've hardly been able to sit still since. I danced around the house, grinning and plotting. I have to find an apartment, some furniture, get a job… Holy F…! – she's coming to Vancouver!!!!

August 27

I called up the group home and got my old job back. That was a relief, and everything else is falling into place. I rented an apartment a few doors away from Kirsten and Leanne in North Vancouver. They are such warm people, and Kirsten is fluent in French which will be good for Anik. Jamie is only three blocks away as well, so we'll be in good company. I know she'll be accepted and they don't have a problem with us being a couple. I told them the whole story and they are dying to meet her. Friends are chipping in and by the time Anik arrives, it looks like we'll have a fully furnished apartment.

It was great to see Jamie today. I missed her so much and had loads to tell her. We had a good chat and a cry over the way "our" trip ended, but all is well. It's amazing really. If we hadn't gone our separate ways in Germany, I wouldn't have traveled (and gotten together) with Anik, and Jamie wouldn't have come home early and gotten her fabulous new job. She said she's hardly drinking, <u>and</u> she's seeing a counsellor (wow and yay!). She dumped Todd soon after she got back, when he confessed that he'd had a fling while she was away. I think it's for the best. She seems really happy. She's looking forward to inducting a new Larry (Anik) into the club.

The Larry of all Larry's will be home next week. Her dad said she's in Turkey right now (way to go Jo!), and she told him to pass some story headlines our way: "Larry gets chased by a bull" and "Larry stands out like a sore thumb marching in local parade". She made her dad write them down, but wouldn't give him any details in case we coerced him into a sneak preview. What a tease!!! I have a feeling she's got a whole list of Larry mishaps to fill us in on. I can't wait to see her!!!

September 2

I met Anik at the airport this afternoon. I was nervous of course but tried hard not to show it. When she walked through the gate, it was like seeing her for the first time – even better in fact, now that my attraction to women has been "set free" so to speak. She is absolutely striking! I couldn't take my eyes off her, and a voice in my head kept asking, "Is she really with me?" I can't believe that she's left her life behind to be with me. I cried happy, grateful tears when we hugged and felt the courage rise up again. I can do this. We can do this. The people who love us will get used to it. Anyone who can't – well I'll be sad about that, but I'd be sadder if I had to deny myself this love. No one should ever have to do that, and I sure won't...

Author's Note

PLEASE FORGIVE THE USE of a pen name and blurry cover photo. For a story about facing your truth and being proud of who you are, it feels utterly inappropriate. I want to share this story in case it can help someone like me, but it's not just my story.

I want to respect the privacy of my friends and family who are included. I especially do not want to shame anyone who has changed and long been forgiven. Not everyone changes when it comes to this topic, and there were some that had to be left behind so that I could be free of their toxic judgement. But those who *did* change have my respect and appreciation. I was not the only one who was judging blindly (in my denial). We grew up in a social and religious culture that interfered with what our hearts might have decided without that influence.

I hope you understand the choice for anonymity. It is not shame or fear. I'm living a proud and happy life now. I hope you are too.

—R.L Parks

www.ingramcontent.com/pod-product-compliance
Lightning Source LLC
Chambersburg PA
CBHW050245120526
44590CB00016B/2217